A Novel

Grassy Water

ANTHONY TIATORIO

Order this book online at www.trafford.com
or email orders@trafford.com

Most Trafford titles are also available at major online book retailers.

Printed in Victoria, BC, Canada.

ISBN: 978-1-4269-2219-0 (Soft)

We at Trafford believe that it is the responsibility of us all, as both individuals and corporations, to make choices that are environmentally and socially sound. You, in turn, are supporting this responsible conduct each time you purchase a Trafford book, or make use of our publishing services. To find out how you are helping, please visit www.trafford.com/responsiblepublishing.html

Our mission is to efficiently provide the world's finest, most comprehensive book publishing service, enabling every author to experience success. To find out how to publish your book, your way, and have it available worldwide, visit us online at www.trafford.com

Trafford rev. 01/14/2009

www.trafford.com

North America & international
toll-free: 1 888 232 4444 (USA & Canada)
phone: 250 383 6864 • fax: 812 355 4082 • email: info@trafford.com

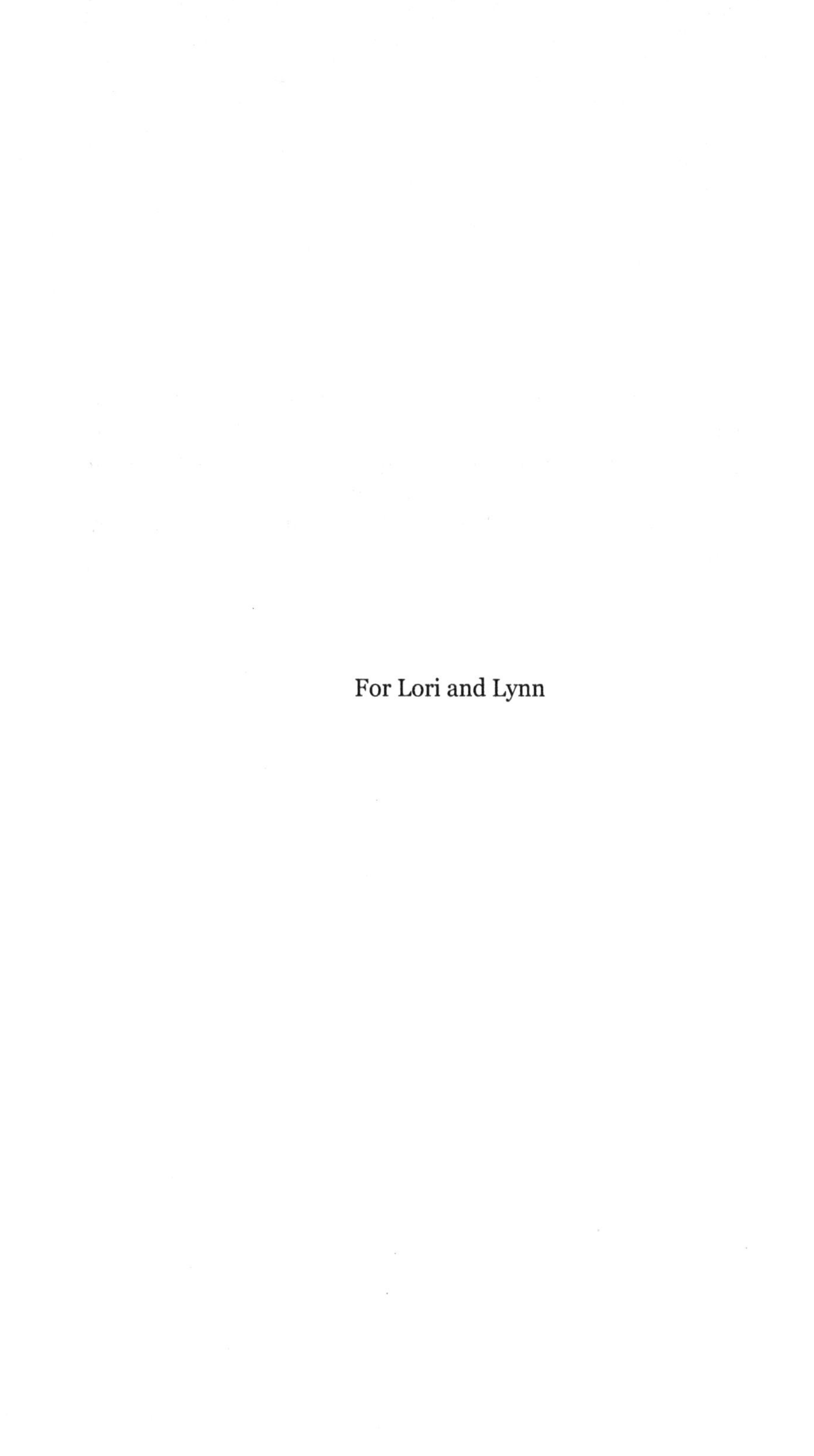

For Lori and Lynn

...The Yalobusha bottom was vast and virgin, a ribbon of fabulously fertile land pressed against the river by abrupt pine ridges fronting endless untamed upland forest. It was, in many ways, a wild wetland jungle where panthers prowled by night and the eerie jutting eyes of alligators silently watched from the watery shadows...

Chapter One

It was Monday evening, December 11, 1882; there was no moon and the snow had already begun to fall. Thomas Hamrick waited impatiently at the Warren Street depot for the tram that would take him into the city. He hated the horse-railroad, especially in winter. It was drafty, cold and uncomfortable in the unheated cars and the few inches of straw loosely strewn on the floor hardly helped. Ordinarily he would know better, but tonight he had little choice. They were waiting for him and it was already getting late.

Thomas was tired and had little enthusiasm for the theater; he never did like Gilbert and Sullivan to begin with, even though their plays were all the rage then. There was something silly about parlor opera he always thought, something self-contradictory, almost incongruous. But, their granddaughter, Anna, was visiting from New York and Amanda had heard so much about Iolanthe, the newest British sensation, which was opening the new Bijou in Boston's blossoming theater district. She wanted very much to make Anna happy and her eighteenth birthday special.

Not only was the play making its long anticipated American debut after several smash weeks in London's posh West End, but the Bijou itself was making its grand opening and for the first time anywhere a theater was to be completely illuminated by electric light bulbs. And it was also advertised that Mr. Edison himself would supervise the event, which was predicted to be spectacular. For Thomas this display of American technological know-how might make it all worthwhile, or at least he hoped that it would.

He masked his rising irritability briefly with thoughts of the wonders of electricity and what it might mean for the future. There were already plans to use its magnetic power to move trolley and street trams and that would be a big improvement over horse-cars he thought, kicking the snow from his boots and peering into the night for some sign of the train. Anything that could reduce the number of animals stabled in the town would be a godsend, if only for eliminating the infernal rotting mountains of manure that rose up beside the corrals and barns.

Then he caught his impatient mind wandering and reminded himself that he wanted to take the Green Line, which went right up Washington Street and made a regular stop at the Adam's House Hotel. The theater was right next door. He hadn't been there since the days of the old Melodeon and his involuntary mind-walk started again. That must have been forty years ago, he mused. The years had passed so quickly. God, he thought, I'm seventy-five years old. Mandy is seventy-two. Where did they all go? But, those had been happy, loving years and that fleeting feeling, for a time at least, lifted his spirit.

"Ya know if they'd let 'em plow the tracks, we wouldn't have this problem," a man beside him said. "But, then the mucky-mucks with their fancy sleighs would be scrapin' bottom... and we wouldn't want that... now would we?"

The man's words reminded Thomas that Amanda had hired a hackney carriage to the theater that night and he wondered how hard it would snow and if there would be service for them after the performance. He could feel the wet, cold north-east breeze blowing steadily off the bay and feared that they could be in for a big storm. Maybe they would have to stay at the Adam's House that night. Maybe they should anyway. But, if they did, then how would his son know? He would worry about them and his young daughter. No, it would be best to get back home.

"Damn it. Where the hell is it?" he blurted and the man beside him laughed and said with obvious disdain, "What a way to run a railroad... even a horse railroad."

Thomas didn't look up, already buried again in his own thoughts. Sometimes he worried that age was finally catching up to him. He couldn't seem to concentrate like he once could. It wasn't that he became confused, just overwhelmed with nuance. There were always more and more factors to consider and angles to account for and the airy linear confidence of youth seemed very far behind him now.

Anna asked, "What's wrong, Mimi?" sensing something, but missing her mark entirely. "It's only a light snow; Bumpa will be fine, you'll see; he'll arrive soon."

"Oh, I know he will, dear. Let's just wait here in the lobby," Amanda answered, only partly masking the uncertainty that had recently barricaded itself in a corner of her mind. She, like her husband of more than a half-century, was slowing down. She enjoyed feeling comfortably settled and wasn't ready to be reminded that the past was never quite over and gone. "Isn't it beautiful? Not stuffy and presumptuous like the theaters in London or Paris, but still very elegant wouldn't you say?" She went on futilely seeking to hide thoughts that had already cemented themselves into her being.

"I can't wait to go up," Anna said. "It's a wonderful birthday present, Mimi, I'm so..."

"And you know it's so much less snobby than in London where everyone dresses to the nines. Don't you think, Anna?" Amanda added without listening.

"I guess so, Mimi, but... then... how would I know," Anna answered smiling, but already beginning to realize that her grandmother was talking aimlessly.

"...and there are no boxes, or only one or two I think. In London there are loads of snobby boxes..."

"You... are worried about Bumpa aren't you, Mimi?" the girl interrupted.

"...and from what I'm told the seats are all in good view. You know that's also a big complaint that people make about the West End."

"What is it Mimi, what's wrong?"

"Oh, look Anna! Signor Brocolini is to play Strephon. They say he was marvelous in..." Amanda tried to push on, but couldn't. Tears welled up in her eyes and, too late to pretend any further, she turned away.

Not trusting her words, Anna stood silently beside her grandmother for a few seconds before the old woman looked up and smiled. “It’s alright, dear. Let’s not spoil your birthday. It was just some old memories from long ago. It’s nothing… really.”

Amanda looked at her granddaughter and thought how much of herself she could see in those eager eighteen year-old eyes, how full of promise the world was then when everything seemed possible and there were rarely any thoughts of regret.

But, the ripple of consequence rolls relentlessly through life, as Amanda well knew. There were problems, recently arisen. She hadn’t yet told Thomas and needed a chance to work it through for herself first. “But this should be a happy day, Anna. It’s your birthday and I don’t want to trouble you.”

“How can I be happy, Mimi, when I see that you’re so sad?”

“You are a sweet child, Anna,” she answered and the caring look on her granddaughter’s face drew her on. “You never knew my brother, Samuel. He was only fifteen when I left him and my mother to come here to Boston with your grandfather. I wasn’t much older than you are now. I wanted to put it all and everyone from my past behind me. It was so awful and embarrassing, what my father had done and then seeing his brutal death. I couldn’t stay there any longer. I never thought about them, about my mother, if she could cope, if Sammy was grown enough to…” The words slowly slipped into an incoherent sob.

Anna held her grandmother’s hand and helped her to a couch in the corner of the lobby. “You don’t have to tell me any more, Mimi. I know about then. My father has talked about it.”

Amanda smiled and squeezed her granddaughter’s hand. “He couldn’t know how I felt or how I feel now. My mother committed suicide, Anna… She was driven somehow to kill herself and I wasn’t there for her. I left her. I didn’t care. I couldn’t face the stares and whispers. I abandoned her when she needed me most. I convinced myself that it was enough that Samuel stayed and then I blamed him when she died. I always blamed him. He was just a boy, but I never forgave him and I never heard from him again. Not until a few days ago.” She took a tattered letter from her purse. It had been read a hundred times without yielding any answers.

“Are you sure you want me to read this, Mimi,” Anna asked, taking the small folded paper from her grandmother’s trembling fingers. Amanda nodded. "Yes dear, I need you to; I must show it to someone."

My Dearest Sister,

I dreamed of a day when I would return, when I would see you again and everything would be forgiven, but I never let that day dawn. Now I fear it may be too late. I have tried so many times to write and to tell you how sorry I am, but those words always seemed so pitiful and empty and so I always chose to wait for a better time. I can wait no longer and do no more than write down my story and hope you will read it and understand.

Please, you must help me now. I have failed my whole life and fear that I will die knowing that I have failed again and in the single thing I most desperately desire. I must be true to my only son. The law has abandoned us. There are powerful and unscrupulous men who have declared him to be illegitimate and therefore unfit to inherit my name.

I am dying and surrounded by treachery. You are my only hope as I shall not survive these next few days. You are my sister, my blood and my sole living heir, as I have so stipulated in my last will and testament. I beg you to do the right thing. Help my boy.

Your unworthy and most remorseful brother,
Sam
Grassy Water, Mississippi
December 1, 1882

"My God, Mimi. What are you going to do?"

"Help him if I can, but I don't know how," she started, her voice slow and steady, but as she spoke her words descended into a sobbing disjointed slur. "He had no one and no one cared. When our older brother was killed, murdered by our own father you could even say, Sammy lost his only anchor. He loved Caleb; idolized him... I should have known my mother wouldn't bear up; she was never strong... I should have stayed after my father's death... I could have held things together... but, I didn't... I thought only about myself and I ran away... my life has been so blessed, Anna... I feel so guilty... I've never seen my mother's grave..."

"What did Bumpa say?"

"I haven't told him anything yet. I wanted to be sure of how I felt first. Then yesterday another letter came, this time from a lawyer telling me Sammy was dead and that I am the heir to his estate. It's a cotton plantation, Anna, somewhere in Mississippi. It's all very complicated and frightening."

"You must tell Bumpa, Mimi. He'll know what to do. Everything will work out for the best, you'll see."

Amanda forced a tired smile. "I hope so, dear."

A voice began, "Ladies and gentlemen you're about to see the future. This, the beautiful new Boston Bijou, is the first theater in America to be entirely lighted by Edison incandescent light bulbs powered by their own independent steam-driven dynamo. Mr. Edison himself supervised the installation of all the fixtures and wiring to power the bulbs and is personally attending the switches for tonight's performance."

"The seats are perfect, Tom," Amanda said, determined to keep everything in its proper order, and hoping he wouldn't notice her reddened eyes. "And the theater is so beautiful, even with only the low light from the chandelier it floods you with a warm almost magical golden glow, doesn't it?"

Thomas struggled to hear over the din of eager applause and waited until it subsided to respond. "Wait until they ignite the proscenium, Mandy and then you'll see what I've been talking about. I read that there are over two-hundred bulbs around the arch. This man Edison is a genius. Apparently he doesn't trust anyone else to handle his equipment."

Amanda's concentration was severely challenged. She tried to listen and managed a mundane response as she struggled to free herself from the earlier unpleasantness. "Why is that, Tom?"

"He has to. There's no one outside of Menlo Park that knows the first thing about electricity. They say he supervises every aspect of his applications. Last year in New York he was even overseeing the digging of ditches and the laying of wire."

When he got no response from his wife, Thomas leaned over toward his granddaughter and whispered, "See those men over there, Anna? They are Edison's men on the lookout for saboteurs."

"Saboteurs," she reacted incredulously. "Who in the world would want to sabotage an electric light?"

"Just think a bit about who stands to lose if this new lighting system really catches on," Thomas replied and waited a few seconds in vain for a response before raising his eyebrows and exclaiming loudly, "the gas company, Anna!"

"Don't yell, Tom. She can hear you," Amanda interrupted with more than a hint of disapproval.

But, even as the chandelier slowly dimmed, Thomas tried to go on, "I heard that they caught a gas-company man in New York, when Edison was demonstrating his dynamo to the Aldermen, who tried to short out the main line."

"Shhhh, Tom, please, tell us later; it's starting."

The house faded to dark and the bulbs arching over the stage roared to life. A low almost moaning sigh of amazement floated up from the audience. "There is no longer any need for footlights, ladies and gentlemen, as the stage is now flooded by Edison incandescent light. Let the show begin!"

Washington Street was teeming as the theaters emptied their throngs onto the snowy sidewalks. The northeast gale that had been feared never came, only a steady gentle snow that covered the city in a cocoon of white. The night was crisp and the first hint of the holiday season only enhanced the already festive mood. For a few minutes at least it lessened and soothed Amanda's apprehension.

The blanket of new fallen snow brought out the hackney sleighs for the first time that year. Brightly colored plumes and flying tassels accented by jingling bells on the backs of prancing horses created a kind of musical carnival that filled the air. It seemed as though the whole world was happy and everyone wanted to slide through the night in a sleigh. Not the waiting carriages of the wealthy, not even a coach and four could match the magic of a dollar ride in an open bob that night.

Amanda saw the delight in her granddaughter's eyes. "Oh, Tom, let's not go right back," she prodded leaning forward from the second seat in the hackney bob-sleigh where she and Thomas were snugly wrapped beneath blankets of fur. "It's such a beautiful night. The sky is breaking clear and the stars are coming out. Wouldn't you like to take a ride first, Anna?"

"Oh, yes. Could we Bumpa?"

Her grandfather nodded his approval and told the driver to, "Take us around through the Common first."

Perhaps it was the location of the bells at that perfect place on the horse's back that caused the melodic clinking counterpoint to the thumping cadence of the trotting hooves. Whatever it was, it worked its wonders on everyone out on the streets of Boston that night. The narrow lanes that crisscrossed the Common were swarming with joyous faces and waves of good will. Anna seemed so pleased that the old couple sat silently, in their own world, content to simply see her smile. It wasn't until they turned for home that anyone spoke and the spell was finally broken.

"You didn't like it, Tom?"

"I don't think it was at the same level with some of their earlier productions... no... Pinafore, for example. The music is very forgettable. Why, I can't remember a single melody."

Amanda went on forcing the conversation, which threatened to become abrasive as it emotionally mixed with the weight of other concerns. "I'm sure Dr. Sullivan was aiming a bit above the jingle level, Tom... what did you think of Signor Brocolini?"

"I don't understand what all the raves are about," Thomas responded. "He has a deep resonant bass... It's true, he sings well enough, yes... But he can't act to save his soul."

"It's light opera, Tom... comedy, not Shakespearean drama."

Thomas was tired. "Oh, is that what it was? Sometimes the lines are just silly, don't you think. Maybe it's me, but I don't get some of this limey humor. Although I must admit I got a good laugh when all the peers of the House of Lords turned into fairies and flitted away."

"Don't mind him, Anna. Your grandfather was more interested in Mr. Edison's light bulbing system than in the play anyway," Amanda reacted cynically. "I swear that's the only reason he came."

"The theater was magnificent though, I will admit that," Thomas offered, easing his tone and smiling.

"Oh, indeed it was. The incandescent light lends such a soft hue that reflects from everywhere. It was positively stunning, almost like being transported into another world. The costumes were so rich and the scenery so realistic, it was so alluring, wouldn't you say, Anna?"

"I thought it was wonderful," Anna responded. "I'm still floating. Thank you so much. I love you both."

"I would have liked it better if there were a more important theme to it," Thomas added, sliding back toward strife, "something beyond mere whimsy. For example, the very idea of a fairy marrying a mortal, isn't that kind of outrageous? How would that compare to say a White person marrying an African? Now we'd have a to-do right here in Boston with that wouldn't we? And we would call the issue of that marriage a mulatto, which is in fact a blend, sort of like mixing cream and coffee. But, this Strephon character is pure fairy down to the waist and then all human below the waist. Now that's strange ..."

"Don't be a bore, Tom, Mr. Gilbert's libretto is not racial commentary; it's comedy."

"But comedy can be deadly serious Amanda and still be comedy. They just don't do anything with it. Now hear me out. Iolanthe married a mortal and by fairy law she must die. Well that's harsh, but when you think about it that's the way it is, wouldn't you say? But, now how is this resolved? Well, since the law condemns to death any fairies that marry mortals, in the end, they simply insert the word don't before marry and now suddenly everything is alright."

"And what's your point, Tom?"

"The point is simple, Mandy. What makes it wrong for a fairy to marry a human, or a Black to marry a White for that matter? Is it really wrong and immoral or is it just a rule that if it were to change would suddenly make it right?"

"It's more than a rule, Tom. It's just not done."
"But it is done, my dear."

Chapter Two

"She was very depressed after that, Tom. She never recovered. Her whole world centered on her husband and she was totally taken apart... Sammy tried to carry on with the boat, but it was no use. He grew more and more resentful of his father and blamed him for everything. Then, when he saw her die in that horrible way... I guess he..."

"Arsenic, wasn't it?" Thomas asked quickly, seeing her about to break down. He had never before dared press too hard on the subject of her mother's death, since he knew that his wife carried considerable guilt herself for not having been there.

"She used it for rat poison. She always had some on the boat. I can still see it there on the shelf, with the skull and crossbones on the label. It gives me the shivers, Tom; I know that's what put the idea into her head."

Thomas said nothing, preferring to tread lightly and let his wife find her own way.

"It was so routine and ordinary, Tom. She was always self-conscious about her skin and even got in the habit of using it as a cosmetic; a lot of women did. She bought it quite openly at the apothecary and had for many years."

"Do they still do that?" he asked trying to divert the conversation away from the deepening darkness he sensed ahead.

"More than ever, I would say. It's hard to tell why though; I don't think it does anything and it makes such a sooty mess. But, beauty you know trumps all. Some women even swallow it, in small doses mind you, thinking they can improve their complexion that way."

"And was that how she did it?" he asked.

"Apparently she took a huge amount. It's a horrible agonizing way to die, Tom. Violent cramping and vomiting and it can take days."

"You don't suppose she blamed herself for what happened and... wanted to suffer? There are certainly easier ways to..."

"Not many, not for women, Tom, not that are sure," Amanda interrupted, not fully dismissing the possibility and wanting to push the thought away. Guilt was a powerful plague in her own mind at that moment.

"Did anyone try to save her?" Thomas asked.

"The doctor wrote me that they tried to get her to drink calf's blood, but she wouldn't. It would probably have been too late anyway."

"Read me the letter again, Mandy, the one from the lawyer, and slowly so I don't miss anything." While his eyes could no longer focus very well on the writing, Thomas's mind was still keen and he searched for any clues in the words.

"Well, of course it's addressed to me and begins..."

Madam:

I am the executor of the last will and testament of Mr. Samuel Olmstead of this county. You are the sole heir and beneficiary of Mr. Olmstead's estate. This letter informs you that the probate hearing will be held in the Court of Chancery at Grenada, Mississippi on June 12, 1883.

There is a legal agreement that precedes and must be discharged before the execution of the will. Mr. Olmstead's partner, a certain Jean Gareau, has a first option to purchase Mr. Olmstead's plantation. This contractual obligation must be met before the disposition of the will and is being exercised. Under Mississippi law, a commission of freeholders has been established to determine the value of the property and it will be purchased by Mr. Gareau at this valuation price. It is my considered opinion that this contract is valid and enforceable. I have therefore decided not to challenge it. I am sure that madam would prefer this, since I doubt that madam wishes to come to Mississippi to run a cotton plantation, particularly one that is run-down and of little real worth. Be assured that you will receive the full cash value of the estate according to the contract.

Please communicate your instructions concerning the transfer of the funds. There is no need to come to Mississippi to dispose of this matter. If madam wishes separate legal representation, I would be pleased to recommend an attorney.

Your faithful servant,

Graham Fly, Esq.
Grenada, Mississippi

Thomas hoped to find an easy answer. “Why not go ahead with it that way then? Give the boy the money and be done with it.”

“That’s not what my brother wants, Tom. He wants his son to get the land.”

“Yes, and that means going down there and fighting this thing in the courts with little chance of winning. It’s not worth it, Mandy. Think of the expense... and for what? He say’s the land is worn out. We don’t even know if the son even wants it.”

Amanda’s emotions were cresting. She faced an almost insurmountable problem in a very far away and strange place and it was one she could not ignore. She had almost no patience or energy to fight on two fronts. “My brother was begging for help, Tom, for God’s sake. He wanted to do the right thing by his son. Can’t you see how driven he was? My father never showed him that he loved him or that he even cared about him. Sammy tried so hard to please him, but he was so cold and distant. He never had a father, really. How can I ignore his dying plea?”

Thomas saw the bottomless need in her tear-filled eyes and knew he had no choice. "Are you sure you want to do this, Mandy? You really want to go to Mississippi and do this?"

The Hamricks rarely saw their only son. The firm had long ago moved to New York City and James had no real business in Boston anymore. Once a year, at Christmas, for a few days, he would come so Anna could visit with her grandparents, but that was it. Her birthday was in December too and it always worked out well. James would only stay one or two nights, saying he couldn't leave this or that pressing matter right then. He would invite them to New York and say that Melissa missed them and wanted them to come and his aging parents would answer that they would try.

Everyone always dressed for dinner on that one special evening and the housekeeper would act as the waitress. There were three courses beginning with the soup. Hilda ceremoniously carried the big tureen from the kitchen and placed it in front of the hostess with the ladle and the soup plates. Amanda prepared the servings and Hilda carried them to each guest. The bread was passed and the tureen quietly taken away.

"Oh it looks marvelous, Mimi. You must teach me the recipe for this."

Anna was first to speak and her father added, "Yes, mother, you've out done yourself again."

"Hilda doesn't usually do this, you know," Amanda protested mildly, "only for this special supper."

The conversation divided along the lines of gender as it usually did and a quiet serenity seemed to fill the room. The old couple was happiest with family all gathered around them.

"Well, first you've got to boil the beef bone. Of course that's done the day before and then when..."

"The advantages are all built from shipping rates. It's the railroads that facilitate the fraud. Rockefeller understood this and negotiated favorable rates that positioned him to squeeze his competitors to either sell out to him or be crushed."

"So you think there's opportunity there, in oil I mean?"

"...and you really need to soak the Shaker corn overnight so that can also..."

"...and that was the basis of the great South Improvement Company scheme, father, the bigger the contract, the cheaper should be the rate."

"...shred the cabbage and add..."

"Yes, James," Thomas reacted, "but the railroads are a public utility. It's wrong for them to give special rates to some and not to others. It's the same as an unfair tax."

"That may be, but the way the price of crude fluctuates, Rockefeller is always looking for a way to control it and hold up the price of refined."

"So he thinks if he monopolizes the refining and is the only buyer he can dictate the price of crude?"

"That's it! The drillers saw this of course and decided to organize a combination to build big storage tanks and hold the oil until they got the price they thought they could live with."

"...you can always add noodles at the end, after straining; they only take twenty minutes and are..."

"Now the shortage is driving up the price on the continent. We've got a ship empty and waiting in New York right now to carry refined to Europe. I expect we'll make a tidy sum."

Next the ham was brought in and placed on the table before the host. Thomas stood and carved the roast, carefully placing several generous juicy slices on the first plate, which was held by the waitress standing by his side. Hilda carried the plate around the table to Amanda who added the vegetables and then the waitress brought the first serving to their son, James. He was always the guest of honor and Thomas loved to listen to him talk about the business, his new plans and investment schemes.

"Rockefeller knows that money rules the roost. Big shipping contracts will sway the mind of any railroad. They'll break any agreement if it's to their advantage. Also he knows that the drillers are too cantankerous to ever stand together for long against him."

"How do we fit in, James? It all seems very problematic and risky."

"Oh, it's risky all right. Rockefeller is dancing on the edge of the law trying to create a legal monopoly, but I'm betting he succeeds. We're going to take a stake in Standard Oil, a small one at first and then see how it goes."

"Don't forget to refill the glasses, Hilda... Oh, and bring more bread... Now as I was saying dear, use a heavy coating of sugar and then baste with sweet cider..."

"If the Standard gets preferential rates from the railroads, he'll drive everyone else into bankruptcy and they know it. Rockefeller got many of the big refiners to turn over their business to Standard Oil in return for stock. This was all done in secret with the intent of bringing ultimately unstoppable pressure on the Pennsylvania Railroad to give even greater preferential rates. It's an octopus that's grabbing everything and hopefully there's still time to get in."

Thomas was hesitant and felt the obligation to voice his concern. "But are these rebates fair and proper, James?"

"Does it matter, father? Millions are being made and I don't see anyway anyone can stop it. Of course there was a push in Congress, and still is, to enact some kind of interstate commerce regulations to bring this thing to a resolution, but nothing yet."

Dearest sister,

This is the memory of my life. I am writing it now so you can know who I have become. Many details are blurry now, particularly from the first years, or have been left out deliberately to save others embarrassment, but the important things, the ones that I think mattered, are there.

"He writes so well, Tom. It's as though he's not the same person from the boy I remember. He always hated books and learning. He seems so different."

Ohio, spring, 1832

The numbers of hogs walking to market was unbelievable. I came at every turn upon endless droves of swine being driven along the roads so as to fill them with animals and glut the bridges, stopping traffic to the unending annoyance of the locals. I was told that forty-thousand hogs crossed the town bridge at Miami that spring. For nearly two months the roads are all but impassable, they become so glutted with animals. I read that there were over twenty million of them in the valley and less than two million were slaughtered each year.

Now, a hog takes two years to grow and fatten, which would seem to show that there were many millions of animals that were not going to market. This I believed was potentially an endlessly profitable business. There was no limit to the corn growing capacity of this rich land. The problem, it seemed to me, was not scarcity of corn but the limited ability to process the meat. The demand for pork was insatiable. Getting it slaughtered and into the barrels was the challenge, and the opportunity. It was as I pondered this that I first saw the old man sitting beside the road, surrounded by a hundred sleeping swine...

"...You driving these animals to Cincinnati?"

"That's right," he responded and seeing Samuel's puzzled expression at the sight of so many hogs lolling aimlessly about added, "they gotta get their rest. Get heat stroke ya know and besides ya don't want to walk too much weight off en 'em."

Samuel wasted no time. "Why would you walk hogs all that way? Why not butcher and pack them closer to home?"

"Packin' 'em ain't the only problem, son. When the season hits they're comin' in hot an' heavy. For two months ya don't see much of anything but hogs in these parts. But ta do 'em ya need cash money, credit money and that means banks; ya need barrels and that means coopers, not ta mention salt. And then ya gotta ship 'em and that means a canal or a river with boats headin' the right way."

Corn was easy to grow in Ohio, but expensive to move. Turning it into pigs right on the farm made good sense and Samuel, in his mind, saw a steady stream of pork, salted and packed in barrels, moving to market.

"What da ya do, boy?"

"Well, I used to sail a boat on Clinton's ditch, but now, I guess I'll do most anything."

"There's plenty o' work in Cinci. It's right on the Ohio ya know. Boats is goin' down to the Mississippi bulgin' with mess pork every day. Them darkies can really put down the fatback and bacon. They don't feed 'em much of anything else I'm told, nothin' but hogs and hominy and what little corn they grow gotta go for that... and the mules too I reckon."

Samuel didn't let on that he had money, quite a lot of it in fact and the idea of making a place for himself in this business was growing in his mind.

"Said ya knew a lot about boats, didn' ya?"

"Canal boats maybe, worked on one all my life. But I never had cause to sail a riverboat."

"Canal boat, river flat, all the same, it's a boat ain't it?"

Samuel and the old man talked for a long time and when the sun began to set he said, "Best be movin'. Wouldn't due to be out afta dark. I'm goin' ta make another mile or two to the next house where I can pen 'em in."

The old man explained to Samuel that just about every farm would take in travelers. Some put up signs saying they were mover's houses to announce to all those going west that they were welcome for the night. "Everybody out here needs cash money," he said. "Even a few dollars a year can make all the difference and there are damned few ways to get it. That's why everybody takes in travelers and Old Hickory's goin' ta sweep Ohio."

The road, which was little more than a rutted trail, ran mostly through the woods and wound its way along the path of least resistance until it met up with the big road to Cincinnati. There was a stage coach on the big road, but, out where they were, nearly everyone walked. Sometimes a man on horseback would be seen, maybe even with a servant riding behind. That man would be accounted well-to-do. Only a rich man could afford a carriage.

Stumps of dead trees stood like gravestones in the clearings and fields of working farms, silhouetted against the orange glow of brush fires on the distant horizon. The smell of smoke was in the air. The smell of smoke was always in the air.

"If the wind kicks up they'll be hell ta pay with those fires," the old man commented. "Them dead trees are as dry as tinder. I seen fires get into 'em, go right up inside the trunk, bust out at the top and light up the night like Christmas candles."

Cutting a settlement into the forest wilderness was no easy matter. Whatever was too big to be grubbed up and burned was deadened by girdling. After the leaves withered and died, the land could be plowed and a crop could be put in right away. The dead skeletons of the once proud hickories and elms stood for decades, slowly dropping before the wind as decay gradually overcame them.

The forest was a blessing as well. Log cabins were just about all there was. Stripped of their bark and flattened on opposite sides the timbers were stacked and notched together. With the spaces chinked and plastered with a mortar of sand and lime they made a remarkably weather-tight house. Openings for doors and windows were cut right through the solid walls and when properly cased and fitted were quite serviceable and handsome. A split shingle roof and brick chimney dressed off the neat exteriors and gave a sense of sameness to the place.

Everyone farmed his own land and dreamed of owning more. "What's it like around here," Samuel asked, searching for a better understanding of the valley and its people. Having come from the political and religious cauldron of western New York, he knew enough to be careful with his words.

"Few's rich and few's poor. Most got just enough."

"What's their politics, I mean."

"Usta all be Scotsmen 'round these parts, Presbyterians. Don't have much politics. Now that the Methodists been eatin' into 'em, they don't have much time ta worry 'bout it neither, too busy arguin' 'bout free will and such..."

The old man's cynical words were all so brutally real for Samuel and forced him to relive the most painful part of his life. He blamed his father's fanatical pursuit of religious causes for his beloved brother Caleb's violent and tragic death and was determined to erase such things forever from his life.

"...now with the Irish Catholics startin' ta pile up like they are..."

"What about politics?" he insisted.

"You'll see a lotta that Jackson craze in Cinci and it's spreadin' out mighty fast..."

...I followed the hogs, so to speak, and they led me to the slaughter and meat packing houses at the end of the line. I determined at that moment to make my fortune in pork, so I set about to learn all I could.

Chapter Three

"It will stain, I know it will. It's black silk, Anna. It's so hard to not bleed it and it's your best evening dress; it's the latest princesse sheath."

"Please don't fret, Mimi. They have new black dyes now you know; they're color tight and don't bleed like they used to."

"Never mind, dear; it's better to be safe than sorry. We need to boil some black kid gloves in water with a little alcohol and then add very soft soap and some honey. Hilda knows exactly what to do."

The housekeeper set to work while Amanda assured her granddaughter that the dress was not ruined. "Once that's cooled we just sponge the silk in it gently until the stain is gone. This will clean it Anna; Hilda will fix it, you'll see."

Anna smiled. Her grandmother's loving concern was so plain and even more touching considering there was no need. "Have you ever heard of Onyx stockings, Mimi?" she asked.

Amanda called after the housekeeper as she carried the delicate treasure to the kitchen. "Don't wring it out, Hilda and be sure to iron it while it's still damp... What did you say, dear?"

"Onyx black silk stockings, have you heard of them?"

"No, dear."

"They're an exclusive at Lord and Taylor's now in the city. They use the new colorfast dyes. Those old problems with silk are a thing of the past."

"Really, dear?"

"You must come visit us in New York, Mimi. Father always asks you and you never come; please say you'll come." When her grandmother didn't respond Anna went on. "I'll take you to Lord and Taylor's big Broadway store, Mimi. It's on Twentieth; it's only a few blocks from us. They have everything, all the latest in French silk crepe from Mesdames Cely and the Maison Morin-Blossier, and the window dressing, Mimi, you must see the windows."

Amanda decided at that moment to do what deep down she always knew she would do. "Alright, dear."

"Alright you will... you'll come?"

Amanda smiled and nodded. "I haven't yet discussed this with your grandfather, but I've decided to go to Mississippi this spring to take care of my brother's business. I'll visit on my way."

"Isn't Bumpa going too?"

"I hope so, dear; I think he will."

"Well... you can't go alone, Mimi."

"And why not?"

"It simply wouldn't do for a lady to travel alone to Mississippi... Mimi... it's the South! A lady is always to be escorted."

Amanda smiled and looked down so her granddaughter wouldn't see the glistening moisture in her eyes. "Don't worry, dear. Your grandfather won't let me go alone; I'm sure of that."

Thoughts of her mother were now dominating Amanda's mind. The world of women always seemed false and ephemeral to her and nothing more so than the penciling of eyebrows and the painting of cheeks. It represented the make-believe world so many, like her mother, lived and died in. Arsenic, she thought, how ironic that it should be the death of so many women and that they obtained it because they believed it would make them more beautiful.

Harriet Olmstead had been utterly of her time and gave credence to the wispy shadow of assumptions that the age had about women, that they were not strong and never sought to face life straight away, but rather relied on stratagem and artifice, preferring manipulation and maneuver to assertive confrontation. But, wasn't this how men wanted them to be and in the end so much of the reason why it was so?

Her mother had lived this role so completely that it gave Amanda cause to conclude that this was what had actually killed her. So much murky intrigue, for so long, living in the world of "what if" and "if only" inevitably generated anxiety that gradually, but relentlessly, turned into raw fear until she was in perpetual terror, spooked by the slightest sound, the dropping of a cup or the barking of a dog. Sometimes the pressure built to where she became hysterical to the point of exhaustion and, like a cloud overloaded with electrical charge needs to explode into violent lightning, she would burst, scream and smash the crockery and glasses to smithereens. And while everyone saw it, no one ever helped her.

"What's wrong, Mimi? Are you alright?" Anna asked, seeing the sadness that had quickly transformed her grandmother's face.

"I'm sorry, dear. It's just that so much has happened so fast."

"You're talking about the letter now, Mimi?" Anna asked.

"My brother is dead. He was all alone and he died and I couldn't reach him in time." The thought of once again doing nothing was more than she could bear. "He sent a kind of memoir, a recollection of his life. It's as though I never knew him. He's so different from what I envisioned. I've missed so much and I feel a part of my life has been lost and I want to know what happened. I started reading it with Bumpa and then suddenly I was afraid."

"I can read it to you, Mimi."

Amanda looked up at her granddaughter and smiled her assent. "I just don't feel comfortable with your grandfather. I don't know what to expect or how he will react and I don't want him to be angry or disappointed in me."

They walked quietly to the master bedroom and closed the door.

I left Cincinnati in 1833 at the close of the winter packing season and at a time when the ice on the great Ohio was breaking sufficiently to allow safe passage south. The opportunity for me to make my fortune immediately arose out of the plight of a Quaker man named Levi Hicks.

Hicks was a riverboat merchant and a pork broker with a contract to deliver six-hundred barrels of ordinary mess pork to some Choctaw Chiefs and Headmen at Vicksburg, Mississippi. He had built the boat and hired a crew, but was unable to obtain credit to buy the pork. The banks, fearful that the Choctaw could not meet their obligation, refused to lend him the money. He faced ruin until I risked half my inheritance and became his partner.

In late April we began drifting down the Ohio. I had great confidence in my skills on a canal, but feared from the start that this undertaking would be beyond them. Our boat was nothing more than a big box, seventy feet long and sixteen wide with four foot high sides, custom built to carry our load. She had thirty-foot oars called sweeps, each worked by two men. Aft was a kind of tiller called a steering-oar. It must have been forty feet long. And, stretching straight out from the bow was another oar called a gouger, which was needed for control in fast water. The whole idea was to simply float downstream, riding the current to our destination, where the cargo would be delivered and the boat broken up and sold for lumber.

There were six men in the crew besides Hicks and me, each of them working for his passage. A big Irishman named Brandon Eagan and his brother Arthur worked one of the sweeps and, as if by perverse design, the other side was manned by two Scots Presbyterians. I don't remember their names. Our steersman was a little Portuguese called Batata and a German they nicknamed Frenchy worked the gouge. Like the boat, they too were all one-way travelers, looking for their fortune in the new government lands opening up in Mississippi...

"...T'ain't much mor'n a raft, a raft with sides, she is," one of the sweepers said as they poled the big barge out into the current.

Descending the Ohio with a flatboat required skill and diligence. The river was full of obstructions, snags and floating logs and brush. It was difficult to navigate and dangerous, particularly at night, when the deep-draft steamboats were constantly swinging left and right to avoid the sandbars at the mouth of every entering river and stream.

"Wear out to the middle," Hicks said assertively, "and watch for General Harrison's plantation. When you see it, get to the channel along the right shore and mind the sand bar. Then wear out to the middle again."

The first rule of flatboat navigation was to never go aground. For the most part that meant following the channel, riding the current and staying away from the shore. There were stretches where a boat could drift for days with hardly any mind. The current swung naturally around the islands and only avoiding the big snags and floating debris required steering.

A few miles ahead the Great Miami entered on the right. "Get along the left shore until we're by it," Hicks commanded, "then wear out again to the middle and stay there."

An awning had been stretched across the boat covering about twenty feet in the stern, creating a kind of makeshift quarterdeck. It was the only protected area and for three weeks they all called it home. The work was mostly little more than lazy lolling around, punctuated by periods of frantic exertion. Killing time with endless political debate was polished into an art form.

Samuel leaned back into the shade and watched the peaceful shore slide past. The majestic Ohio River was bound on both sides by a flat verdant and luxuriant strip of bottom contained in the distance by high hillsides, forest clad. The current, tranquil and placid, contrasted with the strident voices around him. He smiled listening to Frenchy the German, the name seemed so suited to the place and time.

"America can haf no vild people lifing in de middle ov ze land. Dat's zo zimple. Unt belieff me it von't happen. Jackson has right. Die Indianer muss go. Eferybody iss better."

"Well, don't tell me he goes by his own free will," Hicks shot back, his Quaker roots clearly showing. "He's been coerced and intimidated, befriended then betrayed. How can a people willing to die over a tax on tea be so blind and callous as to not see it?"

"Nobody gifs a damn ober die Indianer, Leefei. Vun hears no objections to it vat's going on, becoss der lant iss rich unt golt iss fount!"

"There are some who see the injustice."

"Naa yaa, Calhoun unt Clay, iss hollerin' im Senat, aber das ist only bullshit politik. You know damn vell, Leefei, iss only to slam Andy."

Then one of the Scottish sweepers chimed in. "Do ye not know they've agreed to it? The Indians can plainly see that they're better off goin'. All their chiefs have signed off on it."

The words made Samuel think about the risk he was taking and he worried that the bank may have had better judgment in refusing to back Hicks. He knew the Choctaw had agreed in 1830 to cede the last of their land to the federal government and that most of them had already gone west across the Mississippi. What if they were all gone, he thought?

Hick's voice filtered through. "The Redman has always lived on this land and no twist of logic can justify wresting it away from him by force."

"Verdammt... Leefei, dey hat to dem gut money paid. Die Indianern haben treaties gemacht. Dey fallen unter der gofernments and dey must obey."

"The Indians are children of God who put them here before there were any laws and governments. And it is by the pretensions of these laws that their human dignity is denied."

And so it went for a few more days until they reached the rapids. Frenchy had paddled ahead in the canoe to the landing at Jeffersonville, above the falls, to pick up a pilot to steer them through.

"I thought there was a canal around it?" Samuel asked and Hicks laughed.

"Louisville-Portland Canal, fancy name huh? We don't need it this time of year. Water's high. Ten bucks'll get us a pilot to run the rapids and they want sixty cents a ton to use the locks. We got near eighty tons. You figure it out."

At high water, such as they had, the falls almost disappear, but the river runs faster and underwater obstructions can smash a hull to splinters. It wouldn't do to try it without a pilot. But, as it turned out Samuel worried for nothing. The current swept the big barge along the right channel between Goose Islands and the bank. They came through the falls neatly and smartly crossing to the opposite shore in front of Shippingport they passed the guard lock of the canal feeling mighty smug.

With a canoe to get ashore and back and ample firewood on board it was possible to make the trip nonstop. Lying-to at night was dangerous and not necessary. Keep a watch and stay in the current; that was their plan. Samuel marveled at how effortlessly the boat followed the river around and between the islands, requiring little or no attention from the steersman.

"That bottom slopes up slow to the head of the island," Batata commented. "The current jus' swings 'round 'em and we go with it. But... ya gotta be careful not to get tricked by one of them huge floating snags, made of tangled up timbers and brush, thinking it's a real island. Some of 'em in the Mississippi's so big they fool ya and ya go crashin' right into 'em. There ain't no bottom under 'em and the current don't go 'round, it goes under."

"What about you boys?" Samuel asked the Eagan brothers. "What are you going to do?"

Brandon responded in his strong Irish brogue. "They be after openin' the land office for the new Choctaw territory. Maybe we'll stay awhile," he chuckled, "right Artie?"

Profits possible from land speculation were enormous. Very early in the history of the United States land companies were formed for the purpose of buying and reselling government land. Their pitchmen and posters were everywhere in the towns and cities of the Northeast. The Eagan boys had been planning for a long time and they responded like a practiced duet.

"If ya don't get in there quick ya'll be after losin' out, ta be shur."

"Speculators'll gobble it all up, they will. The federals there, I wancha ta know, they like ta sell big chunks o' land, all at once."

"They do be after talkin' 'bout the Yazoo bamboozle, ta be shur."

"Damn near sold off the whole o' Mississippi, they did."

"Speculatin' devils just sit back and get rich, never step a foot on anythin' they buy. Get it for a dollar an acre and they be after sellin' it for four, that's their motto, tiz."

"What the devil makes the land worth anythin' anyway if it's not the plough and man behind it, I say?"

"We gonna beat 'em this time, right Artie? We goin' deep in the delta, we are."

At the mouth of the Ohio, being careful to stay left, opposite the town of Cairo to avoid the bar, they carried effortlessly into the Big Muddy.

The upper Mississippi is plagued by some different perils. Again, riding the current is best and the rule is still to stay away from the shore. The banks are very loose and tend to collapse without warning causing erratic currents and difficult to read conditions. Water can suddenly break through a low bank and rush out at any point creating an explosively fast flow sucking everything it catches out of the main river and into the swamps and bayous beside it.

And, it wouldn't do to stop and lie-to below a high bank either. The weight of trees growing right up to the river's edge, coupled with soft soil, can cause a bank to collapse instantly, burying a boat with everyone in it beneath an avalanche of roots and mud.

After his mother's death Samuel brought his boat to the western end of the Erie Canal and sold it along with every other thing he had inherited. He was determined to erase all ties with his past and to follow his dream, the dream he had shared so often with his brother, Caleb, to go west and make his fortune. He deposited his money in a Buffalo bank, engaged an agent and boarded a steamboat for Cleveland, carrying a few hundred dollars and thousands more in negotiable letters of exchange. As he crossed Ohio he soon discovered that in this cash strapped country, dependent on credit, the bank was king... and that he was a bank. Opportunities abounded. He only need find the right one. But, did he? This thought festered in his mind for days. He couldn't escape the fear that he would lose everything. "Tell me more about what's happening down there, Mr. Hicks. This intense interest in getting Indian lands is driving this whole thing, I think."

"The Choctaws gave up some really good territory in Mississippi already. It started ten or fifteen years ago. But, that first Choctaw cession really wasn't selling too fast. There was always demand from speculators, but the move to push the rest of the Indians out was more political than economic."

"I'm concerned about our investment, Mr. Hicks. I can't afford to have it fall through."

"Well you know what happened to them was the Indians were settling into farming and improving the land and the Whites got scared that they would set up a separate country right in the middle of them so to speak. So they passed new state laws to put the Indian lands under the Mississippi government."

"Don't these Indian tribes have treaties with the United States?"

"Those treaties aren't worth a plugged nickel unless the President is willing to enforce them. The Indians had a case to be sure, but with Jackson elected there was no way. It didn't matter what happened in the courts. Everybody knew Jackson wanted the Indians out... all of them, and in the end that's the way it would be. The Choctaw got the message that's all. They were afraid they'd lose everything. It was either make a deal with Jackson or try to fight Mississippi. So, hell... they signed another treaty a couple of years ago to trade the rest of their territory for land west of the Mississippi River, in Oklahoma."

"Well if they've gone to Oklahoma, Mr. Hicks, who do we deliver this pork to?"

"They were supposed to go in three stages. The first two, in 1831 and then in 1832, have already gone. The last of them are set to leave this summer. Like I told you, we got our contract with one of their chiefs, Philippe Robidoux. But you never know who you're dealing with. They ain't like regular governments, there are different groups and chiefs and headmen. Nobody speaks for them all."

"This Robidoux doesn't sound like a Choctaw Indian to me."

"There's a lot of mixed blood among them, especially with the Cajuns from down in Louisiana. A lot of times it's hard to tell you're talking to an Indian. There's a lot a sharks and flimflammers too that'll even scam their own people, but I don't see any way this..."

"So you're sure the deal is good?"

"They have to eat. There's a long trek ahead of them. And we do have a bit of a guarantee. All the Choctaw debt is now the responsibility of the federal government."

"Well... that's good to..."

"... but it means we have to deliver before we get our money and there'll be a delay getting it... But we'll get it; I'm sure we'll get it."

CHAPTER FOUR

We reached Vicksburg in late June and delivered our cargo. As expected we were not paid and were told to present our bill to the receiver of public monies at the newly established land office, in a place called Chocchuma, several miles away at the edge of the recent Choctaw land cession. It was then that I parted ways with Levi Hicks. As I had financed the entire pork purchase and he had provided the boat, it was agreed that he would keep all the proceeds from the sale of lumber and that I would pay him two-hundred dollars and recoup what I could from the federal government.

Chocchuma was little more than a few tents in a clearing on the banks of a river called Yalobusha, but already hundreds of land-hungry men had gathered there to await the sale of Choctaw land that was scheduled to begin in late October. It was to grow into a boomtown of shacks and saloons, inns and brothels, before the whole business ended in 1842.

I had a claim for over four-thousand dollars and to settle the debt I was offered two sections of unimproved land of my choosing. This was twelve-hundred and eighty acres, a tremendous tract, but one which I would be unable to sell without incurring a steep loss since an acre in the Choctaw cession was expected to bring only one or two dollars. My only thought at that moment was to secure my deed and hold on to it until the value of the land rose. The first step was to hire a guide to help me select the best possible place...

"...Bout eleven, ten year ago I say, Jean Gareau, when you don't gotta move on den what you went for? And he done said, Jean Gareau, you half Choctaw Indian an' you entitle ta land... really and truly. An' dis here feller what toll me dat well he'd like ta die ya know when ol Jean Gareau lay claim ta his land. An dat's for true."

Jean Gareau was a Cajun Choctaw who had suddenly found his native roots, over a decade earlier, in 1820, when he learned of the terms of the Treaty of Doak's Stand. This had been one of a series of Choctaw land transfers and any man not wishing to relocate was entitled to claim a section of land as his own. He would not however receive deed to the claim until he had lived on it and improved it. Jean Gareau selected his six-hundred and forty acres along the south bank of the Yalobusha River at the northern edge of the first Choctaw cession. But his rights remained incomplete to that day, with only a stilted shack in a swampy bayou and a whisky-still to show for his meager industry.

Samuel was completely beyond his depth and desperate for help. There was something likeable and safe-seeming about the tragically poetic Cajun and so he decided to take a chance. "And you say you know these woods and will take me back there to stake a good claim?"

"I can't help but thought 'bout goin' back dere, me. Bout dem bayou, an dem gator an dem moon she shinin' bright in de black a night. I'm push away de thought... till now dat is. A lotta peoples dey rightly die, dey would, for what I got back dere, me... I garontee. An what you got, too. Iffin you want it dat is."

Gareau told Samuel that the Yalobusha River was the line separating this new land hand-over from the earlier one that he had been part of. His claim was on the south bank of the river, at the furthest extent of navigable water; and the land was rich. He told Samuel that if he claimed his piece on the north side, together they would control both banks at the uppermost deep water point. It would be the last stop up the Yalobusha, even for the smallest steamboats and would dominate commerce out to the Yazoo and the Mississippi below that.

"Don't know sometime what bed I's sleepin', me. I can't stood dat no mo. Dis time ol Jean Gareau don't drop da potata. We go all down da bayou an I show ya, really and truly."

"At the same time that they signed agreements guaranteeing no discount in rate would be given to any shipper, the New York Central signed an agreement with Rockefeller to give him twenty-five cents off on every barrel! Of course it all had to be kept quiet."

"Why would they do that, James?" Thomas could tell how much his son enjoyed talking about his plans and remembered how much it meant to him to have his own father listen. He didn't see his only son very much anymore and he wanted James to know that he was proud of him and of his accomplishments. "You'll have to fill me in on all of this. I'm afraid I'm falling out of touch."

"Look at what Rockefeller offered to them, enough carloads of oil everyday to make up a whole train. That cut the costs colossally by eliminating the need to deal with mixed freight and multiple shippers. Plus the fact that, from Cleveland, the Standard could ship by other roads, or by water even. He had the Central at his mercy, and of course they didn't give a rat's ass about breaking their word not to do it. Rockefeller just started to squeeze everybody. They either sold out or they got snuffed out."

Thomas knew exactly where to insert a comment. "It seems to me that Rockefeller's biggest problem would be the drillers."

"You're right, Papa! They were his most natural enemy since he had to buy from them."

"More Madeira?" Thomas asked, reaching for the decanter and knowing that the story was far from over.

"Please..." James nodded and paused briefly before continuing. "His basic strategy was to hold back refined until he drove down the price of crude. Of course while he was stocking refined, crude was piling up behind it. The oil men didn't have the tanks to hold it and in the end they caved. They were hoping that the

Empire Pipeline would save them, but when Rockefeller just went ahead and bought it they began to get the picture. They would never get a drop of oil out of the fields without him!"

At that moment Amanda's voice caught their attention. "Please, I don't mean to interrupt, but Anna and I have decided to take our tea in the parlor while you two talk."

"Oh... I'm sorry, mother; I'll stop..."

"No, you go on dear. I know how much your father misses this sort of thing," Amanda smiled and then turning to her granddaughter said, "Hilda is preparing jasmine tea. We have it right from China."

"Isn't it frightfully expensive, Mimi?"

"But it's so good, Anna; it has a musky kind of smoky character from the jasmine and a very strong tea flavor. Come dear, we'll use the Chinese porcelain as well."

The gentlemen stood while the ladies departed and waited until the door had closed before resuming their conversation. "An old friend of ours is still in the China trade, somehow he gets it out of Hang-chow and he always brings us some. But, go on, James."

"The drillers were making a mad dash to find a way out, build their own pipeline and more storage tanks, but the oil was piling up incredibly. When the Bradford Field was discovered it was plain that there would be an even bigger flood of oil. You know where that led. In no time the drillers were forced to take whatever Rockefeller offered or run their oil on the ground."

"Aren't the railroads and even the pipeline, for that matter, common carriers that under the law can't discriminate?" Thomas repeated his earlier observation.

"Yes, you're right and the other refiners finally brought suit against the Standard... and the railroads... claiming that they conspired to drive them out, but they withdrew the suit when Rockefeller promised to stop his discriminatory practices. You'd have thought they would know better having dealt with him before, but apparently they never learned. Of course he had a new plan up his sleeve to corner the entire oil market, this time with a trust idea."

"A trust?"

"Yes."

"Interesting choice of words wouldn't you say?"

"Indeed!"

"I still don't understand where our firm fits in James. It seems like a very risky business to get involved in."

"Well... yes, but... let me tell you about this trust idea...

"They'll be at it for hours, Anna. It's so wonderful to see your grandfather's eyes light up when he talks to your father. He misses the business deeply."

"I love this tea, Mimi. I've never had it before. It's so different."

"Isn't it good? Somehow they infuse the tea leaves with the fragrance of the jasmine flowers."

"When I was a little girl, papa took us to Charleston one spring and I remember sitting on the veranda and it was just covered with jasmine. The scent wafted over us, sifting through the Spanish moss drooping down from the big oaks that hung over the house... and the climbing roses, Mimi, blooming on the wrought iron fences. It was so romantic. It must have been wonderful to live in the South back before the war, more genteel, almost like feudal times..."

At that moment Amanda's mind filled uncontrollably with thoughts of her brother, difficult and sometimes sad thoughts and she hardly noticed the innocence of inexperience flowing from her granddaughter's lips. "...and the ladies riding right along side the gentlemen on morning hunting parties and the formal dinners later and the dresses... Mimi, can't you just see them in their beautiful gowns as they strolled through the lush gardens."

"What did you say, dear?"

"It must have been like a never ending dream, Mimi. The women were so refined it seems, cultivated you might say in the arts and music and so skilled at conversation... I wish I were witty."

"You're a beautiful young woman, Anna and every bit as clever as any southern belle."

"I do wish you would let me go with you, Mimi. I've never been anywhere and it sounds like such fun!"

Amanda had no daughters of her own. She treasured the all too little time she spent with Anna and for a fleeting moment she rejoiced in the thought that it would be fun and she felt happy, rekindling memories of giggles and girl talk. Then just as suddenly she put it away. "They've had hard times down there of late, Anna. Since the so-called Republican Reconstruction ended there's been turmoil, racial turmoil. I'm not sure it's safe... with the Ku Klux Klan and all."

"Oh Mimi, don't be silly, in what possible way could we get mixed up with the Ku Klux Klan?"

"I don't know, dear, but there are problems and until we know what they are I think we should be very cautious."

"Then we'd better read more of Uncle Samuel's memoir."

We traveled east up a narrow road along the south bank of what Gareau called the Bouge Loosa. It was little more than a trail and no wagon had ever passed over it. The trek was harrowing at times as the heavy seasonal rains had washed away the bank in many places causing the surface to suddenly plunge into the river.

The bottomland was wide and well drained, being cut by numerous sloughs and bayous, which however made it difficult to cross on foot, particularly in the wet season. Gareau told me that the soil was a loose yellow loam, so profusely fertile that rich yields of corn could be had without even plowing it. Just push the seed into the ground and watch it grow he said with infectious enthusiasm.

We walked all day, minding our steps and there was no other soul to be seen. When we reached the spot and I gazed along the river, stretching away from me, all I could see was forest. The thick stands of willow, chestnut, cypress and oak were endless. I couldn't help thinking how ironic it was that the demand for lumber was so acute in the midst of all this virgin woodland. But, of course it was the lack of labor; it was always about labor.

Night was falling when Gareau led me into a cypress break that backed against the river's edge. After a few hundred yards it settled into a bayou where he had hidden a canoe, cleverly tucked among the standing roots...

...The Yalobusha bottom was vast and virgin, a ribbon of fabulously fertile land pressed against the river by abrupt pine ridges fronting endless untamed upland forest. It was in many ways a wild wetland jungle where panthers prowled by night and the eerie jutting eyes of alligators silently watched from the watery shadows.

The swampy still green of the placid grassy water blended seamlessly with the moss covered cypress trunks that stretched upward to reach the setting sun. There was a damp swelter to the air that hung heavy and wet on their skin. The small canoe glided almost effortlessly, avoiding the tangles and rotted stumps still stuck deep in the muck of an ancient muddy bottom. Deeper and deeper they slid into what seemed to Samuel to be another world, conjured up from the primeval past. Somehow he sensed that it was the place of his destiny. "Where are we headed?" he asked showing some uneasiness as darkness began to cover them.

"Dis away. Bout a half-hour up da bayou. You be seein' somethin' mighty good... not now, but pretty soon."

An alligator silently slid past them and Gareau smiled seeing a hint of fear flash across Samuel's face. "Let me tell ya somethin'. Ya don't go foolin' wit dem gator ya know. He'd like ta ate ya, he would, an sometime dey will."

Samuel didn't yet know it, but Jean Gareau had a dream too, a dream that he now saw a way to reach. Carving a cotton plantation into the wilderness was never a matter for brute force alone. It always required investment capital; Gareau had none and although he knew cotton and possessed a square mile of the richest land in America he could do little more than survive on it. He lived as best he could from the natural bounty of the forest, with fishing lines, snares and traps. The only cash money he could earn came from a small whiskey still. And, of late he drank more than he sold. But then, as Samuel would soon learn, Jean Gareau had more than a dream... he also had a plan.

"Dere it is," Gareau said triumphantly as the canoe came to rest against the rotting hull of an old boat, hopelessly mired in the mud and roots. "Drug it in myself, me, didn't hab dem mule neither. Dat's far as she went and dat's for true."

It was an old steam launch, no more than thirty feet long that had gone aground exploring up the river, years earlier and was abandoned. Gareau had spent months digging it out and getting it into the bayou. He told Samuel that they were in the middle of a massive cypress break that grew right into that bayou and it would be possible to adapt the walking beam on the steamboat engine to power an up-and-down saw blade and make a sawmill. Logs could be floated right up to it. Cypress boards and planks could easily be gotten out down the river and were in great demand all across the South. It was cash money waiting to be had.

They spent that night in the Cajun's bayou shack and Gareau poured out his plan, along with his moonshine whiskey. It was a poor man's plan built entirely on sweat, but it had a touch of genius to it and stood a real chance to succeed. The key was the homemade saw mill, which would allow them to profit from the clearing of land, raise money to buy mules, seed and tools to get in a crop of cotton. Once that cotton came in, it could be turned to cash and more land cleared and more cotton planted, and on and on... Samuel was intrigued and beginning to get excited.

But the plan had a flaw and the flaw was potentially fatal. Cutting and moving the timber could not be done by one or even two men and that meant that slaves needed to be bought, housed and fed for months before any income could be expected. Cabins had to be built for them, saws and axes bought and the steamboat converted into a sawmill. All of this was impossible without money.

"Dis here is what dey call shickin gumbo, an allowin' I don't got dem shickin, you gonna get catfish gumbo. Soon as I get some hot on dat dere. It be only bacon fat wit sausage, hot pepper, onyon, garlic and flour. When dat be all brown like dat we gonna fill dat pot wit some a dat water, some a dat whisky you bin keepin' your eye pealed on, little bit a salt an dem big chunks a catfish."

Gareau's eyes gleamed as he outlined every detail attending the planting of a cotton plantation into the wilderness. He told Samuel why it was as important to grow Indian corn and raise pigs as it was to grow cotton and how crop rotation meant two seasons of cotton then one of Indian corn and that it was not possible to allow a field to lie fallow because of serious erosion problems from the torrential rains that would likely occur. Samuel knew nothing about farming, much less cotton farming in Mississippi, but slowly, listening to the Cajun Choctaw, it began to seem possible and he imagined himself as a plantation owner.

He masked his revulsion at becoming a slave master with hatred for his abolitionist father. In fact, more than any other single thing, openly rejecting everything his father had stood for, drove him to embrace Gareau's scheme.

"Woo... now look at dat... ooo ya... dere's some mighty good shickin gumbo wit onyon, I garontee. Only dere be no shickin in it."

Two men as different on the outside as any two men could be wove their dreams together that night in the bayou. It would be too much to imply that they became friends, but true to say that they understood each other.

"I be jus a young mahn, me. I guess, like you, 'bout twenty when I brung myself here. Dere's a lotta things what I gotta did, but I never done no wrong ta nobody. I live pretty good. Usta be better den now though. Liza she die lass year. A genuine lady woman, she was."

Samuel said nothing, but he knew the depth of being alone and what it meant to be lonely. The two men ate gumbo, drank whiskey and talked until dawn. Samuel learned about the sand bars on the Yalobusha and how to navigate them and how the Loosha-Scoona flowed in above them and would likely cause floods in the wet season, but that the bayous drained the bottom well and besides his land was on the north bank and not so susceptible. Later the next day Samuel Olmstead staked his claim.

"We better went ta Natchez an' bought dem slave."

Chapter Five

"We thought we might take the steamer down to Charleston and then there's a rail connection to Grenada, Mississippi. That's where that lawyer is," Thomas remarked as he studied the standard railroad map and timetables with his son.

"It's a long way to go, just to get to Grenada; there's a change in Grand Junction, Tennessee and no Pullman service on it," James pointed out, studying the schedule from over his father's shoulder.

"Won't there be rest stops?" Amanda asked.

"Yes, there will, mother, but you'll definitely have to overnight in a hotel when you reach Grand Junction. I'm sure it will be slow and exhausting."

James was worried about this trip. His mother and father were getting older and the details were very vague. He wanted to know more and felt responsible for the safety of his aging parents. He was determined to protect them, but careful not to seem overbearing. "I don't know, first the boat to Charleston, then that slow train... I think you should go straight through non-stop... Look here," James began again, running his finger along the lists of arrivals and departures, "There's a fast train with Pullman daily from the Pennsylvania depot in Jersey City straight to Nashville via Cincinnati. From there the Mississippi and Tennessee Railroad goes right through Grenada on its way to Jackson."

"And you think we should use this... Pullman service?" Amanda asked.

"Absolutely, mother," James responded, quickly jumping at the chance to give guidance. "It's the latest convenience. The

Pullman parlor cars convert to sleepers for the overnight; they have a well stocked buffet and porters to deal with the baggage. It's close to a thousand miles you know from New York City to Nashville. Pullman would be the most pleasant and comfortable way to go, I think."

"That is a long way, Mandy," Thomas agreed, "and we'll be in New York anyway..."

"Will it be hard to change trains, dear? We've never done this you know."

"There's nothing to be afraid of, mother. Even in the big stations all the tracks and trains are clearly marked. If it's too busy and you get confused, the Pullman conductor will see to it that you don't go off the wrong way. You can even arrange to have your bags brought right to your hotel room."

"I'm sure we'll manage," Thomas protested, feeling some measure of insult at the idea that his son seemed to imply that he would get confused trying to read the signs in a railroad station. "We're not senile, yet."

"I didn't mean it that way, father, but we are concerned about you two going so far by yourselves. You are getting on you know."

"I'll go with you," Anna burst out, turning to her grandmother and finding the perfect moment to introduce the idea indirectly to her father. "There's a ticket office right near us on Broadway. Any agent can book us through and reserve hotel rooms by telegram. I'll have it all done for you."

"Well... I don't know dear. Of course we'd love to have you come, but that will be up to your father," Amanda responded cautiously, not revealing that this had already been schemed. "I would feel safer though," she added, turning toward her granddaughter with a knowing look.

"May I, Papa?" Anna implored after a perfect pause.

"I don't see why your father would object," Thomas tagged right on cue. "You'll be with us."

"Oh, please, Papa and I do want to go."

James smiled and nodded his head approvingly, acknowledging that he had been over-matched. "I think that probably would be a good idea."

At that moment the housekeeper interrupted to announce the arrival of Luther Loomis, the family attorney.

"Please show him in Hilda," Amanda responded. "We asked Mr. Loomis to advise us, James and we'd like you and Anna to stay and help us as well."

They adjourned to the parlor where Loomis instructed them at some length on the process of probate and then duly disclaimed any knowledge of Mississippi laws, strongly recommending that they retain a local lawyer to represent them. "I can make some inquiries if you would like, but I really..."

"I'll have our attorney in New York recommend someone," James interjected, recognizing the lawyer's obvious efforts to extricate himself from the case.

"That probably would be..." Loomis began again, but Amanda, whose mind was moving rapidly, interrupted.

"What about this option to buy the plantation, Luther, does that sound proper?" She was having difficulty understanding her brother's apparent fear that his son would be unjustly deprived of his rightful inheritance and was becoming increasingly suspicious.

"If it's an enforceable contract, as Fly says, yes... it will have to be dealt with before the estate can be inherited, as he said."

"My brother sent me a memoir, Mr. Loomis, telling his life story and there is no mention of any partnership or agreement or anything like that with this man named Jean Gareau. They worked together at first, that's true, but I don't think they were ever actual business partners. I'm almost certain that there's something going on. If this were the problem my brother would have said so."

"There must be some basis for the man's claim, Mrs. Hamrick and it will have to be presented to the court, hopefully a written document, signed and witnessed. When you get down there, talk to Fly. If you're not satisfied, hire an attorney to represent you, a Mississippi lawyer, and have him look at it. There's not much we can do from here."

Later that evening, after Loomis had gone, James asked to see the memoir. "I read it all the first night with your father and then Anna and I have been rereading it slowly, trying not to miss anything," Amanda said, handing the loosely bound manuscript to her son.

"And doesn't he tell you exactly what this is about?" James asked, apparently taken aback.

She raised her eyebrows and shook her head slowly. "He said I would learn more, but then we got the letter from the lawyer informing us of his death. Bewildering isn't it?"

"Mystifying I would say," James agreed. "So all we have to go on is the memoir?"

"Yes."

"Then I guess we'd better have at it," James responded with a soft smile that comforted his mother who, with her family around her, finally stopped being afraid that she would be left alone to cope with the perplexing strain of it all.

"Anna dear, would you read for us?"

We arrived at Natchez landing late on a Sunday morning and I was immediately amazed by the number of steamboats arriving and departing. Hundreds of Negro porters and draymen, slaves from nearby plantations working for wages on their so-called day of rest, were sweating and singing, as they loaded and unloaded all manner of freight. The levee was lined with flatboats, their crews carousing about, laughing and swilling whiskey while watching the comings and goings along the landing. Stores and grog shops were all open. It was a profane swarm of humanity normally unheard of on the Sabbath and only made possible by the need of so many Blacks to work for short money on that day.

The importance of Natchez landing to the river trade could easily be deduced from the number of cheap taverns and inns in the low town along the levee and the fancy hotel in the high town on the hill above us for the respectable planters and their families seeking passage on the dozens of steamboats that stopped there each day. Natchez was also the slave trading center of this region and it was the slave auction that brought the two towns together.

Slaves were bought and sold privately and sometimes in public auctions all across Mississippi, but Natchez dominated the professional trade of the so-called commission agents, who would ship and store any kind of merchandise, including Negroes. Their advertisements appeared in the newspapers and on broadsides; the competition between them was often intense. For that reason we at first believed that a private sale might offer us the best opportunity.

Gareau insisted that Kentucky Negroes were most reliable and least likely to be damaged so we thought to contact the agents receiving slaves from there. While they all preferred private arrangements and claimed fresh offerings arriving daily and the lowest prices for lots, sight unseen, it was clear that each slave needed to be carefully selected individually. The public sale was our only alternative, so we decided to attend the auction of the firm of W. F. White & Co. of Lexington, Kentucky that claimed to have a well stocked slave depot...

...A few buyers and dozens of onlookers gathered in the lobby of the Parker Hotel that Monday morning. It was hazy from tobacco smoke and the smell of sweat. Dozens of slaves were sitting along the wall, reaching back into the hallway. They each had a numbered ticket tacked to their tattered clothing. Bidders were given a corresponding list with a brief description of each lot and Samuel was relieved by the opportunity to look down at it while he sorted through his thoughts.

1. Mattie-Lou, 19, prime young woman.
2. John, 31, prime cotton hand.
   Katy, 25, cotton, unsound, has fits.
   Silky, 6.

Kate, 3mos.
Jake, 13, prime boy.
3. Noble, 41, cotton, lame in one leg.
4. Joe, 49, rice, ruptured.
5. Cassius, 31, prime cotton hand.
Luna, 30 prime woman.
Cassius Jr., 11, prime boy.
Jonas, 7.
6. Mary, 40, rice hand.

It was as unlikely an occurrence as could have been imagined, Samuel Olmstead buying slaves. He was, in fact, the son of a fanatical abolitionist and had been taught almost from birth to despise everything about the slave-holding South. How could he be here now... doing this?

"No..." he screamed silently to himself. "My father was a worthless son-of-a-bitch, a murdering bastard; I spit on his grave."

Samuel had driven away this demon many times and was relieved by the auctioneer's voice. "Gentleman... W. F. White & Co. of Lexington, Kentucky offers at auction a large and well selected stock of slaves, fully guaranteed and sold for no fault."

The slaves were to be presented in lots and it would be sometime before they reached the Kentucky field-hands he and Gareau had come to buy. Samuel was surprised by how many of these Negroes had distinct European features and light complexions. One woman appeared to have no African blood at all and many were young mothers with children. He looked at one described as fourteen years old and to be sold with her infant son; she was holding him in her arms. It made him alert to how often he saw words like "breeding slave" or "child bearing woman" in the descriptions he was hiding in.

And then it started. "This is Mattie-Lou, 19, prime young woman. How much for this likely girl? She is sound and warranted so. Look her over. What am I bid? Who will pay seven-hundred dollars?"

The man next to Samuel stomped his cane loudly, again and again. "She's a comely one alright, but yo caint tell nothin' till y'all get a closer look."

"By God, y'all know yo cain't never tell how old dese po Nigro girls are," another man added laughing, "'especially quadroons like this heah one." Several men gathered around the young woman, playfully pressing in on her and having what they thought of as fun. "Yo gotta feal the body for the firmness of muscle and fleash; it's ouwa way."

It was a routine of torment endured by pretty young girls and Mattie-Lou knew it all too well. She closed her eyes and stiffened her back determined to stand her ground, when suddenly Samuel yelled, "one-thousand dollars, after a closer look."

"Step away you men," the auctioneer quickly commanded. "The gentleman bids one-thousand dollars upon approval. Get back and let him through."

Within seconds Samuel had bought his first slave. It wasn't what he had expected, or what he came for.

"What you done dat for?" Gareau complained. "Don't go buyin' dem single female womans. Dey don't swung dem axe. We need dem big bucks. Now you let Jean Gareau show ya how dat's did!"

The slaves were all advertised as flawless, but few were. Most had some kind of defect as it was called. This was usually disclosed or discovered on the auction block. Most of the individual field hands that Gareau hoped to find had them, an awkwardly healed bone fracture, missing fingers, the loss of an eye or part of an ear. To Samuel, these were all indications of abuse and even torture. But, Gareau took a different clue from it, having nothing to do with the apparent cruelty. He saw it only as a sign of punishment and a warning that the slave would be unruly and difficult to control. The Cajun Choctaw was very careful about this and it seriously limited his choices. In the end he settled on three field hands and two small families. They bought eleven slaves in Natchez that day, five men, three women and three children.

"How is she, Mandy?"

"I put her to bed with a swallow of Lydia Pinkham's. She's tired that's all, complaining about backache and some cramping, typical women's weakness as they say."

"It sounded like she was crying."

"She'll be alright," Amanda answered assertively.

"Do you think we should call Dr. Higginbotham? I'm sure he'll come out in the morning," Thomas pressed.

"I don't think she will consent to see him, Tom."

"Why not, she's ill isn't she?"

"There's no need to call the doctor," she reinforced in a tone meant to end the discussion.

"And you really think that will help, the Pinkham's, I mean?" Thomas changed direction having learned long ago not to involve himself too deeply in the mysterious realm of women's troubles.

"Lydia E. Pinkham's Vegetable Compound most certainly will help, Tom. I've known Lydia for years; long before she became so famous, we all swore by it and urged her to start selling it."

"She certainly has made a go of that. It's in all the pharmacies across the country and I'm told she has a regular factory up there in Lynn."

"And for good reason, Tom, it works!"

"Dr. Higginbotham says it's all the alcohol in it that makes the women forget their troubles. I hope that's not why you still drink it at your age," he added trying to bring levity to a subject that he should have sensed irritated her deeply.

"He would say something like that, Tom. The medical profession doesn't take us seriously. It's no wonder that women don't trust doctors and turn to other women, like Lydia. Did you know that she gets hundreds of letters each month from women all across the country who feel abandoned by their doctors?"

"That's a bit harsh, wouldn't you say?"

"Good God, Tom, some of them are removing the ovaries to cure menstrual cramps!"

Thomas still failed to realize the seriousness of this issue for Amanda and how it was mingling with and intensifying other concerns. He tried again to lighten the conversation. "It's the corsets I tell you. All that pressure squeezing down, it displaces the organs and that's what does it."

"You know, Tom, for all your flippancy, I believe for once you're right. Only it's not the corsets, it's what the corsets symbolize." In over a half-century Amanda had not been able to quiet the anger she felt at the manner of her mother's death. She tried not to, but it was a way to lessen her own feelings of guilt, so, in the end, she blamed her father and with him, in general, all men.

"Dare I ask?" he responded.

"Because beauty is so important to women, for so many it's their only source of admiration and happiness. It's the false male image of women that rules them. Why do you think so many female complaints... nervousness, dizziness, cramping, backaches, are thought to have their origin in the womb. It's an obsession that ruins our lives."

"Higginbotham says that women don't tell the truth to their doctors and don't reveal the full extent of their problems. How can the doctor cure the patient if the patient lies to him?"

"Dr. Higginbotham is a fool, Tom. Women are made by this society to be so protective of their fragile femininity that they cannot bear to admit any flaws or weaknesses peculiar to their sex, especially to men. It is truly tormenting for a sensitive and refined woman to answer questions of that sort from a man, even a physician. And an innocent young unmarried woman like Anna would never go to a male doctor with her problems. Women need help from other women who understand women."

"And that would be Lydia Pinkham," Tom answered with a broad smile, feeling put in his place although not quite understanding why. "I hear she's not well," he went on trying again to ease away from the tension.

"Yes, poor thing. She isn't well at all. I really should visit her again."

"We'll go as soon as the weather warms." Thomas seized the chance to change the subject. "On our way we can stop in Revere. I've been keen to see the big new ocean pier they just built at the beach. It goes out for a quarter-mile and it's all roofed with pavilions and restaurants, far cry from when we first took the train up there." Thomas sensed that his wife wasn't listening and started again. "Do you remember when we would go up to the beach in the summer? We'd take that narrow gauge right along the shore."

"Why do thoughts of the past sometimes give us so much pleasure and other times so much pain?" she reflected. "We seem addicted to constantly reliving our lives and judging... Why are we always judging?"

Her suddenly serious demeanor caught him by surprise and he paused before responding. Thomas knew the root of it all and that more talk would not pay any dividends, only being there would help. "That's just the way we are, Mandy. We just need to stop ourselves from allowing the past to destroy our future."

Chapter Six

For three months we all lived together in wall tents and cut lumber in the cypress brake on Gareau's side of the river. There was a sense of purpose and shared destiny to it that seemed to inspire everyone.

The sturdy little sawmill proved worthy and we slowly began to build a balance with the factor agent at Vicksburg, although our need for provisions, especially bacon and Indian corn, put exceedingly heavy burdens on that. By autumn, cabins had been built for a slave quarters, the kitchen-house was up, the gin-house and the press were built and the main house was well under way. We had a ferry-raft connecting the two sides, a barn for plows and tools and a stable for the six mules that I bought with the last of my cash money.

All that winter was devoted to cutting trees and burning brush to get the land ready for the first crop. This was a rough and wasteful rape of the forest, but there was no other way. Trees had to be got rid of to open fields for plowing. What logs we could get into the water and to the mill were cut into boards and planks to be sold. But, hundreds of majestic oaks, magnolias and hickories were brutally girdled and left to die.

By April we were able to plow and seed sixty acres into cotton. The soil was already naturally fertile and we added all the ash we could get from the fires. Even with the stumps and root-tangled clods that would for years mercilessly harass our plows, we reaped over four-hundred pounds per acre that first year.

The road was utterly useless for wagons as the rain rudely washed it away into huge ruts and gullies. Getting our cotton to market was only possible by the river; fortunately we had a good landing. We floated those early bales out with the lumber on simple timber rafts, at first to Grenada, which was growing into a significant place, and sometimes all the way to Vicksburg.

The price of clean cotton was very high in the early years, but even at twelve cents and more a pound, it didn't bring nearly enough. It was quickly clear that I would need at least four-hundred acres under cotton and another two-hundred in corn to make the plantation profitable and that would take decades of work and many more slaves.

The amount of cotton that can be got to market is limited by the number of hands that can be put to picking it. It takes twice the work to harvest as it does to plant and cultivate. When the season comes, every grown man and woman goes to the fields and I came gradually to appreciate the wisdom of Gareau's insistence that first day in Natchez that we buy young families as the natural increase in population is a generous source of income.

By the time the war came fifty-six slaves were at Grassy Water and I had a two-story comfortable wood-shingled house of sawn cypress filled with fine furniture. It had a big veranda covered by wisteria and lush gardens in front for cutting flowers with a fruit orchard of plum and peach.

The trunks of the dead trees that for so long gave a sad and desolate look to the landscape had finally rotted and fallen. The roots and stumps were nearly all gone from the open fields, which were mostly fenced now and protected from the dairy cattle by thick brambles of Cherokee rose. The land had truly undergone a metamorphosis, as did my own life after the birth of our son...

...Masses of flowering Chinaberry trees swept away from the big house into the slave quarters. They grew thick along the cow barn and in their dense shade a small stone-lined cellar had been dug in the cool ground to hold the milk. Samuel never locked or guarded the bulkhead door because milk was plentiful at Grassy Water. The health of the babies and small children was always uppermost in his mind. As the demand for cotton rose, so did the need for labor and up with it went the price of slaves. Raising strong healthy children was a key to economic survival.

"De boss say no chilluns can wuk 'til dere eight year ol' an youz eight year ol' now." The strong growl of the big Blackman's voice sent a chill through the little body. Then a broad disarming smile told the boy that everything would be alright. "Roun' heah chillun's firs' chores is helpin' Mammy Viney."

Uncle Cassius had been with Samuel since the first day at Natchez. He and Luna had five sons working the fields; three were born at Grassy Water. He was Samuel's most trusted slave and his duties were all encompassing. "Sometime yo' gonna tote water and wood to da kitchen. But now, Mammy Viney gonna teach ya how ta milk da cows. It's a heap o' wuk milkin' dem cows an' Mammy Viney need all da help she can git."

There were six cows at Grassy Water and two at least were always milking. That meant fifteen gallons or more a day and the children had all they could drink, whenever they wanted it. Any left over was churned to butter. This seemed to some to be an extravagance since several acres of the best land had to be put into turnips and buying hay was very costly. But, without healthy children to sustain it, Samuel knew his plantation would surely be doomed. He didn't think of this as a rejection of his own past, but that's precisely what it was.

He was born and raised on a canal boat and from the age of seven he had skinned his father's mules on the towpath beside the Erie Canal. He had no real childhood, never lived in a proper house and rarely felt happy or even safe. Now he had land and roots, a wife and son that he loved deeply, a purpose in life that inspired him, yet none of this could mask the lingering fear that in the end he would lose it all.

Mammy Viney looked down over her apron at the little boy. "Dis heah be a cow an' her name be Moonie. Right now Marsa gotta bull too, but yo' chilluns doan go nowhere neah no bull... We gotta milk dis heah cow two time ebry day. Mammy Viney do it when da bugle blow while all yo' chilluns be sleepin'. Den roun' sundown it be yo' turn whilse Mammy Viney be busy in da kitchen."

To a small child, a cow is a massive hulking beast. There is something monstrous and mechanical about the abrupt angularity of the bones that evokes images of a huge menacing machine capable of moving awkwardly in any direction and this made the warm damp living whoosh of air from the hairy nostrils even more worrisome. Even the swift fly-chasing sweep and thump of the tail was spooky. But... the big wet lip-licking tongue was really scary, and Mammy Viney's next words were truly terrifying. "Yo' gonna give 'er a kiss and tella yo' lov's 'er."

Now, Moonie's long wet tongue was prehensile. It could grasp and pull up big bunches of strong tall grass with ease and she loved to wrap it around little faces, lapping them from the neck to the forehead in one warm wet slather, while exhaling a misty gust of fermenting hay. That was precisely why Mammy Viney always chose Moonie to meet the children.

"Yo' talk ta 'er now an' tell 'er yo' loves 'er. 'Cause iffin she don't like yo' she won't give nuffin'."

Squeaking out "I luv yo', Moonie" through the extreme corners of the mouth at lightning speed without leaving the slightest crack that might be found by the huge wet tongue was a skill quickly mastered by every child placed in the care of this faithful and affectionate woman.

"Now we goes to da udder end." She loved this joke and laughed out load while the little boy looked forlorn.

"Open yo' peepers chile an' look straight ahead dere at dat udder. Dat's full a milk and we gonna git it out."

Now the bulging little eyes were focused on the huge straining sack of milk that seemed about to burst and the four long puffy teats hanging down.

"We got ta git it... all out... cause tamorra she only make what we take taday. Keep takin' less an' less, keep gittin' less an' less, til ya git nuffin' 'tall. Now chile yo' watch ol' Mammy Viney and see how she do."

The old woman pulled her stool up and sat down. Pushing the cow's leg aside to make room, she began firmly caressing and massaging the heavy bag of milk. "Yo' Moonie, sweet Moonie, I's gonna milk yo' now. An' when dat milk be all gone yo' gonna feel sooo good, Moonie. Now yo' jus lax and chew some a dat cawn and lasses dat I brung yo' an don't pay Mammy Viney no mind." Then she gently wiped off the udder with a clean cloth and in moments warm milk began streaming down, left, right, left, right, the rhythm of squeezes and splashes went on until the bucket was nearly full.

"Yo' turn now, boy," she said locking her victim between her knees. "See dem teats dere? Take hole a dat pap in yo' hand. Hold on ta it. It aint gonna bite."

Mamma Viney put her hand over his. "Now squeeze it down like dat and when a little milk come, rub it all over dem teats and make 'em slippry and smooth."

In a matter of minutes the boy was milking with both hands, hardly realizing that he was on his own and he didn't see the warm smile on Mammy Viney's face as she backed off the stool and pulled him up onto the seat. "Now I doan wanna see no chuckin' an' pluckin' on dem paps dere. Yo' gotta go gentle like an' when yo' do she jus be standin' dere smilin' an' chewin' dat cud... an' when yo' gits ta da end... dat las bit a milk is dubly good, warm an fresh an all yourn."

Anna and her father had gone home to spend the holidays with family and friends in Manhattan and the old couple were alone on Christmas Eve. They dressed for dinner as they always had. The table was set and the turkey roasted with all the trimmings, the tree festooned with decorations and, as was their recent practice, they planned to attend the Christmas Eve performance of the Messiah at the Music Hall.

They sipped their wine and talked again about frozen turkeys and about why Thomas always insisted on raising his own bird. Amanda knew why he did this but he told her again that you couldn't trust that the frozen store-bought bird wasn't left over from last year. They ship them in now from God knows where he said and she tried to listen again about how the Christmas goose is the custom in England and that it wouldn't be patriotic to follow that tradition, so eating the noble American turkey is the right thing to do. When he looked up he knew she had been crying.

"What's wrong, Mandy?" he asked reaching across the table to touch her hand.

"It seems so empty, Tom," she said softly. "Where is the joy of Christmas without children?"

"But, James is grown and gone now Mandy, that's all. Isn't it enough to know that he is happy?"

"I can't help thinking about the poor... children, Tom. Christmas seems so sad for them."

"We give what we can..."

"Why do we always donate five dollars, Tom, to buy Christmas dinner for a poor family?" she interrupted with a little anger in her voice. "Why do we feel good about that and never give any thought to what comes after that?"

He felt compelled to say something and began, "Well, I guess that's..." but she wasn't yet through.

"It's not the dinner that will make them happy, the poor little things, it's the gifts that they wait patiently for, but never get and the toys they pray for, call up the chimney to Santa Claus for, the toys that never come."

Thomas was still at a loss and fell back into the safety of dispassionate analysis. "Poverty will always be with us, Mandy. It's the natural state of things."

"It's not just poverty anymore, Tom. It's evil now and it strikes me as depraved. They say that adversity strengthens the character and makes one stronger, but I fail to see how this kind of poverty can do that. It seems so debilitating and destructive to me. It's growing everywhere in the slums, out in Lowell and the other mill towns, even here in Boston, and it's destroying so many children."

"It's the sweating system," he began, eager to escape the emotional vice that seemed to have taken hold of his wife and return to the safer world of reason. "It makes the use of child labor easy and convenient."

She listened intently to every word as he explained how the sweatshop was a parasite on industrial society that thrives wherever poverty is prevalent and need great, and how it clusters in the cities and festers in the tenement buildings where it preys on the children of immigrants. It's very difficult to control, he said, because it's hard to find. Workers have little contact with each other and rarely complain. The dishonesty of the factory owners is matched by the hunger of poor families and the result is an unholy alliance that abuses children who are routinely herded into unsanitary and dangerous jobs.

What do they do and how does it work she asked and he told her it was a system of jobbing out piecework to be done at home or in makeshift workshops set up in tenement buildings. This work is contracted out by factory owners to middlemen who then find the workers to do it. The income from the labor that went to pay the contractor was said to be sweated out of wages that should belong to the worker. It creates an underclass of paupers dependent for their survival on their own oppression.

"But what do they do, Tom." She insisted. "What do the children do?"

"They sew buttons or make artificial flowers. Anything that requires repetitive drudgery and little skill suits the exploitation of children, Mandy."

"There was a time when a child was a child, Tom. Where do they play, in the darkened corridors and narrow courtyards of these sprawling tenements? How does a child grow up with the street for a playground? Can't the parents see this?"

"They think putting their children to work increases their income, but it in fact does just the reverse don't you see? They depress their own wages and drive themselves deeper and deeper into poverty."

Suddenly her posh evening at the Music Hall seemed wrong, even immoral to her. "I want to see it, Tom. I can't bear to go to the concert. I want to see the poor."

"They're giving a Christmas dinner for the lonely tonight at the Tremont Street Methodist. I guess we could go there."

"No, Tom. I want to really see it; I want to see the tenements."

The Boston she first knew had changed. Foreign-born immigrants now made up almost one-third of the population. The Irish were everywhere and lately there had been an influx of Jews from Russia, mostly along Salem Street. The once fashionable North End, particularly along Hanover, between it and Commercial, near the freight yard, was now packed tight with boarding houses and low rent flats, separated only by narrow alleys leading to tiny courtyards and dingy light shafts.

She shuttered, startled at the slamming of the saloon door in the alley beside her and quickly turned to see a small boy, hardly more than six, sliding through the shadows along the blackened brick wall. His little body bent into the cold wind, as he struggled to carry home a heavy jug of beer. In the distance she could hear the off-key strains of a bad brass band and slurred voices singing a mocking yuletide cheer.

They followed the boy without thinking or talking until he turned into another menacing alley to an unmarked windowless ironclad door. He stopped as though sensing them there behind him, but then suddenly pushed with all of his weight though the barrier and into a dark dirty hallway. Then three flights up rickety wooden steps along the tattered wall, through a narrow unlit passageway cluttered with rags and trash, higher and deeper they went into the murky despair of the tenement. Surely the creaking floor betrayed them, but still the boy didn't turn, not until he reached the door. He paused, then opened it and without a word walked slowly in. He didn't look back or close the gaping entrance, yet he had to know that they were there.

The orange glow of a tiny candle dimly lit the sad scene within. They saw the split wood stacked everywhere and felt the irony of the corner workbench covered with cloth daisies. The smell of sooty smoke from the leaking chimney pipe hung in the musky air. In the middle of the one room apartment several small children huddled for warmth close to the rusty woodstove, while a woman, holding an infant, wrinkled and tired beyond her years, stirred their Christmas cabbage and potatoes. Three mattresses and piles of rags were lying along the back wall and a man, half clad, looked up from there.

"Where the hell you bin boy?" he slurred, reaching for the crock of brew.

The old couple stood silently, out of sight in the pitch-black of the hallway and held their breath when the squinting man peered in their direction. "Why you leavin' that door open boy?" he yelled. "If you ain't the stupidest..."

"He just forgot is all," the women interrupted. "Go close it now before your father..."

"But... how will Santee Claus...?"

"Shhh, now you never mind 'bout that. Close the door tight. We're goin' to eat supper now."

CHAPTER SEVEN

Grant rolled his Yankee army right down the Mississippi Central line into the heart of the Confederacy in December of 1862. They tore up the railroad yards and tracks in Grenada, burning all the rolling stock, commandeering every horse and mule that could be found. Nearly all the farms were abandoned, their owners fled south by the thousands, and more thousands of Blacks went north through the Union lines.

Then, when the tip of the dagger was pointing right at the politicians in Jackson, they got scared and, just before Christmas, the governor began issuing proclamations creating emergency militia companies in every county to help the army resist the invasion.

He ordered all men and boys between sixteen and sixty immediately pressed into military service and called upon every loyal patriotic person to comb the woods and swamps and apprehend anyone who went into hiding. But, by that time, Grassy Water was already behind the Union lines and we were all effectively out of it, thank God.

The Yankee soldiers swarmed like locusts, stripped out everything they could carry and at first delighted in destroying the capacity of the farms to produce a new crop come spring. They seemed bent on little more than some sort of revenge until they realized what the cotton was worth and then everything changed. The price had reached fifty cents a pound and was rising.

It wasn't long before the Mississippi river was in Yankee hands all the way out to the gulf and around here the whole war effort seemed diverted into black market cotton trafficking. Huge fortunes could be quickly made as northern speculators were eager to pay big for it and high ranking military officers were all too ready to be bribed for permits to ship it out of the occupied areas.

This caused more than a little confusion until Lincoln finally put the whole business of cotton trade under the authority of treasury agents and the army was told to get the planters to take the loyalty oath and put their farms back into regular production. As I had always opposed secession and was a transplanted northerner myself, I was one of the first to take the oath.

After they got the news about being free, some of my slaves ran off, but Luna and Cassius and their boys stayed. Even then we had a miserable time at first getting any of the newly freed men to come to work for us. I offered them good wages, but they seemed content to be idle. That may have been understandable to some, after all those years in slavery, but it didn't square with the Yankees who wanted a cotton crop that summer.

Orders came in and the army clamped down hard on any freed men who were just hanging around with no job or prospect of getting one. They were told in no uncertain terms to go to work or be drafted into labor brigades for the war and marched south. After that we had no trouble signing men to labor contracts. In fact, until the end of the war we had more hands than we needed.

That last year of war was the most profitable ever at Grassy Water. Production was good and the price was very high. But, I paid dearly in other ways for it and I fear that I'm paying for it still.

It seemed to me that most of the planters north of Jackson, to survive the times, fell in quick enough with the Yankees, but after the war ended it was hard to find any to admit they weren't forced into it. When the reconstruction came everybody took sides and some of us had no choice but to admit to what we actually were, scalawags...

"...The wah is over. Ouah armies were overwhelmed by brute fo'ce a numbers. The butcher Grant, satyr that he is, knew enough not to insult the honah of ouah brave soldiers at Appomattox because he feared they would fight to the death of evera man rather than sully the honah of the South." The speaker was momentarily halted by the rising roar of stomping canes and boot heels. Tensions were very high as the old planters returned to claim their land and rebuild their fortunes. Meetings were held in every town and crossroads as the old order tried to gain control of the future.

As the crowd began to quiet, he started again, raising his voice to reach above the din. "It is mah great pleasure to introduce to you ouah own hero of that lost cause, with the fervent hope the he can lead us out of this Yankee hell." Again the enthusiastic thumping of applause stopped him.

Samuel had reached the lobby of the Planter's Hotel in Grenada, which was packed with people, overflowing into the street. Even the women came out in great numbers. Elections were about to be held, critical elections, dangerous elections, because for the first time former slaves were going to vote. Candidates had to be found and a campaign organized to keep the carpetbag Republicans and their scalawag lapdogs from taking over the state, or at least that was the prevalent mood that day.

Samuel found himself pressed by the crowd into a loose discussion together with some local acquaintances, among them an old friend, Judge Joseph Johnston. Mrs. Johnston was speaking and heads were bent inward to hear.

"Whah he is a baboon, aw suwear, or an orang-o-tang or ha-ever they say it. Aw do declare aw have never seen such a hairy human. And why did he want to take ouah slaves away from us? They were ouar property, after all. I truly do not understand any of it... I suwear they wish ta destroy ouah culture because we are so supeariah to the mongrel North."

The conversation was suddenly interrupted when a man began violently stomping his cane. "By God, it's Olmstead. You dare show your face here, sir?" Frustrations were high and the man was seething with anger. "You are a traitor, sir and always were a Yankee polecat. If I were a young man, sir, I would beat you senseless."

The judge stepped between Samuel and the intruder with a glare in his eye that, although he said nothing, instantly defused the confrontation. Samuel had known the Judge and Mrs. Johnston for many years and could sense that their friendship had been severely strained by his actions during the war; the wounds were raw and would not easily mend. He knew that his lack of loyalty to the Confederate cause was deeply resented, but he was determined to stand his ground, he couldn't hide and he had nowhere else to go.

"Good morning, sir, and how's your good lady?" Samuel reoriented himself politely trying to put the unpleasantness behind him. He turned and quietly bowed to Mrs. Johnston, but she didn't offer her hand. He smiled and turned back to the judge. "Are you well, sir?"

The judge exhaled through closed lips, puffing his cheeks, shook his head and said, "Do you think this is wise... coming here today?"

"I never took up arms against the South," Thomas reacted angrily. "I just stayed out of it. It's over now; I think it's time to move on."

"I was against it myself, Olmstead," the judge answered with an intent frown. "I knew it would mean disaster and a certain end to slavery. But, once the war started I had to stay loyal to my state and stand by my neighbors and friends. You betrayed them and there are many in these parts who are determined to make you regret it."

The judge's wife was furious, her eyes widened as she struggled to remain dignified and ladylike. "And when the butcher had his heel on ouer throat, Mr. Olmstead, you all helped them against we all..." Her anger rose almost uncontrollably as she saw the look of denial on his face. "I know you did, sir... We all do..." Regaining her composure she finished in her nastiest tone. "Please enlighten me. I do not understand whah you love the Nigras so."

"And you did well enough too by God, sir," The judge added feeling the need to support his wife. "That's plain to see and there are those here about that can see it very well." The judge was angry at his old friend, but then in a softer tone gave assurance that despite it all he would not be abandoned. "Secession was a mistake, Samuel; I know that. Everybody knows that. But nobody around here is going to admit it."

It was probably true that the South would have eventually faced emancipation, but gradually and with time to adjust, not this way. The war created a cataclysmic restructuring of society that no one was ready for, White or Black. There was an immediate and confused need sweeping the South to blame someone or something for the catastrophe and it focused on the rush into secession and saw the early Confederate leadership as hotheaded and foolhardy. But, even that was trumped by Samuel's sin of disloyalty.

"What will happen now?" another woman asked. "Who will take care of them. The po things are like children; they caint take care of themselves. You know that, Mr. Olmstead... You'll see; we'll have them on ouah hands again. They caint help what they are, po' dears."

"They'll have to pay for them, that's all." a man asserted, although he knew it was only a dream. "There's no other way. They were our property for God's sake."

Former slaves all over the South were feeling the promise of freedom and refusing to work while holding to their own false hopes about forty acres and a mule. They were both wrong and with the end of forced wartime work contracts even Grassy Water was facing a vexing labor crisis.

Mrs. Johnston had calmed herself and not wanting to part on such harsh terms said, "Whah don't your Yankee friends just leave us be, Mr. Olmstead? They don't understand ouah ways an they want ta steal ouah property from us. Whah I believe they've done it already with some federal laws or some kind of amendment..."

The direct rail link from Boston to New York City, called the Shore Line, was nearly seamless now, save for the ferries across the Thames and Connecticut Rivers and even then it would be considerably quicker than transferring to the steamboat at Stonington as Thomas and Amanda had customarily done. Since, this time, they were going on to Mississippi, it also seemed wise to let the railroad porters deliver their extra luggage directly to their son's fashionable brownstone on the west side near the park.

Their first step out from under the portico of the new Grand Central Depot plunged them into a confusing hectic blur of noise and clutter. Throngs of impatient commuters were flowing past them into the street, turning left and right, intent on getting quickly to wherever they were going. The little black one-horse hackney cabs, lined up like miniature hearses all along Forty-Second Street and up Fourth Avenue, were filling one after the other. The drivers, perched high on white omnibuses, parked in every possible place, were hocking their destinations and routes and the cross-town streetcar, shuttling passengers to the Sixth Avenue elevated station, barely had room to pass.

The city had nearly tripled in population since the Civil War and was beginning to burst at the seams. It was a volatile, but vibrant, mix of immigrant labor and capitalist investment that was quickly becoming the most important commercial and manufacturing metropolis in the world.

But... it was also a dirty and dangerous place, with the world's highest mortality rate and where half of the children under two died of disease. By that spring, New York City was literally suffocating in filth. Over fifty thousand horses dumped tons of manure and rivers of urine daily into the streets, and it was difficult to cross town without encountering the carcass of a dead animal.

"Look at this Mandy, it's incredible. How does he live in a place like this?" Thomas said, feeling the jostle of bodies pushing past him. "There's a restaurant across the street there, maybe we..."

"James said to wait here, Tom," Amanda interrupted, looking left and right along the street. "We don't want him to have to hunt all over for us."

Just as Thomas was about to protest they heard, "Bumpa, Mimi, here we are... over here."

The old couple tried to sort out the confusion. "Over here, Mimi..."

"There they are!" Thomas reacted pointing toward an approaching carriage and recognizing a smiling face leaning out.

"Help your grandmother, Anna," James said as he came quickly around to open the door for his parents and signaled to the driver of the two horse open hackney carriage to hold steady. Within a few seconds they were all in and on their way.

"Would you like to look around the town, Papa?" James asked.

"I don't think so, James; we were here only a couple of years ago."

"This city changes like the wind," his son responded. "And now the new elevated railroad is really boosting development uptown. Land prices are going through the roof."

"No... your mother must be exhausted," Thomas persisted.

"Oh... Mimi, you've got to ride the el," Anna exclaimed. "It runs way up north on third and sixth. It has cute little steam engines, Mimi... Papa... drop us...

"Your grandmother is tired, Anna. I'm sure she'd rather not."

"Another time, dear, I'd love to see it, really," Amanda said, not wanting to disappoint her granddaughter, but dreading the need to climb so many stairs just to ride in another train.

"Well, we're going under it anyway," Anna reacted with only a hint of disappointment. "You can see it at least," she added and then suddenly, "Don't forget to pick up the linens, Papa!"

James turned to his father, "We do need to make one stop at the laundry. It will only take a few minutes."

"You use a steam laundry, James?" Thomas asked.

"No, actually we started using a Chinese hand laundry... Ping-Ming's it's called. It's just across town a bit, on thirty-ninth. They're springing up all over the city."

"Chinese?"

"There are a lot of Chinese here now, a whole throng down on Mott Street, and these hand laundries are starting to open all over. The trouble is they don't deliver. But the work is excellent and it's cheap. You'll see."

"Don't you think steam is better? I mean less chance of spreading germs?" Thomas asked.

"All the washing is done by hand, but the water is very hot, almost boiling. The white things and linens are definitely disinfected. Besides, the dirty clothes never cross the clean."

"What do they do with the colored things and flannels?" Amanda asked. "Surely they don't boil them."

"Well, no, but everything is ironed and that is sufficient, or so I've been assured."

The front of Ping Wing's shop was divided by a partition with the soiled washing taken in over one counter, marked, sorted and gathered in wicker baskets. The clean laundry, ironed, folded, wrapped with paper and labeled, was delivered from another. James presented his ticket at the out counter and a man quickly retrieved his laundry, after which James said very slowly and deliberately, "This gentleman would like to see your shop. He is looking for someone to do his washing."

At first the man didn't respond and James repeated, pointing to his father, "This man want washee washee. Want look-see."

The man smiled, nodding vigorously and said, "Ah so, you come dis side. Lookee see, allo plopa."

Behind the first partition the space was divided into a kind of assembly line with three small rooms, one for washing, a second for drying and a third for ironing. A man was scrubbing clothes on a table with a stiff brush, while another paddled the boiling wash in a large copper kettle. "Seem-washee, you pay plenty dolla. Ping-Wing han-washee, number one chop," the man went on. "Lookee see allo velly plopa."

Thomas wanted to ask some questions, but knew that it would be difficult and he was rapidly becoming distressed by the extreme heat and lack of ventilation. A big wood stove was roaring in the center of the drying room and clothes were hanging on lines along all the walls. A heavy damp dead air closed in on him and he began to feel weak.

"You walkee... chop chop," the man said, sensing Thomas's discomfort and ushering them out of the drying room to where another worker was busy at a long table whisking water on the dried clean clothes before ironing them. "You see... Ping-Wing velly ploper... number one chop."

Thomas noticed several bunk beds along the wall in the back and a man cooking food on a small stove. "You walkee, chop chop," the man repeated nervously and Thomas was relieved to reach the cool air of the street.

"I thought the Chinese immigration was halted last year. Didn't they pass a law?" Thomas asked.

"Yes, but they're still coming in, more than ever I think. This country needs labor and the Chinaman will work hard for very little pay. As long as there's a job for them, they'll keep coming."

"You know, James, I heard Dennis Kearney's speech a couple of years ago at Faneuil Hall. He drew a huge crowd and he seemed to be drumming up what he called a working man's movement against immigration, especially Chinese."

"That doesn't seem like you, father," James queried.

"Well, Ben Butler was getting set to run for governor and his people asked me to support him and this Greenback Party, which I was curious about... so, I knew Kearney was stumping for Butler... so I thought I'd go see."

"What did you think?"

"More of the same tripe about conspiracies among capitalists to control the money supply. It doesn't seem like much has changed since Jackson. Only Kearney ties the money monopoly plot in with cheap immigrant labor, particularly Chinese, undercutting the White American worker. He calls them coolie slaves and sees some kind of grand cabal trying to take over everything."

"So I take it you didn't join the Greenback Party," James chuckled, but his father was serious.

"It did seem ironic that Kearney gets so much support among the Irish," he remarked reflectively and then added ambivalently, "They do seem kind of like slaves though, those Chinese laundrymen, I mean."

"Now, you, sound like Kearney," James quipped again. "You know the White working man in this country has always railed against cheap labor, first slavery, then free Blacks, now Chinese immigrants. They're all lumped together as enemies of the true American working man."

"I didn't mean it that way, more on the human level. Those men were sleeping and eating right in that stifling hole where they work."

"And they do it without complaining. That's why they're so attractive to their bosses. Middleman agents smuggle them in, work them sixteen hours a day, six or even seven days a week; they sleep and eat right on the premises and they are happy to get the job. They don't spend any money and go back to China in a year or two with a few dollars in their pocket. It all feeds off of poverty and oppression in their homeland that drives them to desperation and the fact that we're willing to exploit them."

"You seem to like it," Thomas challenged. "Aren't you part of the problem?"

"The work is good and the price is low. How do you turn it down?"

"Why did Congress ban Chinese immigration then, if the work is good and the price is low, that is?"

"It's just politics," James responded. "The political pressure in California got the law against the Chinese passed. You know about a fourth of the labor force in California is already Chinese and the Whites put up quite a stink. But, that's just political theater I think, because they're still coming in and no one is really trying to stop it. It's wink-wink, nod-nod between the politicians and the big money boys."

"As long as the work is good and the price is low," Thomas added with a wink and a nod.

Chapter Eight

Lower Broadway, where fashionable showrooms and department stores lured shoppers and where the country's rich came to buy the best, was already cleverly called Ladies' Mile. It was the birth of America's gilded age and people-watching rose into an art form. Young men cruised the streets in private carriages and ogled the elegant ladies as they strolled, bustles swaying, gazing in the elaborate display windows along the sidewalks. Outdoor street vendors hawked wares of every description and store greeters announced sales and bargains waiting just inside every doorway.

And there was a growing middleclass with money to spend as well that rode the el down Sixth Avenue to the Fourteenth Street station to shop just across the street at Macy's or took the cross-town omnibus at eighth to E.J. Denning and Co. where five floors, filled with every description of dry good, covered an entire block between ninth and tenth. But, Anna and her grandmother went straight to the premier upscale department store destination of the day, Lord and Taylor.

"It's Rue de la Paix, Mimi, absolutely the latest and finest lingerie and very expensive. Are you sure you want to?"

"Of course dear; this is for your bridal trousseau, don't forget," her grandmother responded warmly as the two women examined some of the imported French fashions at Lord and Taylor's store on the corner of twentieth and Broadway. Chinese silk crepe was in high vogue on the continent and Lord and Taylor boasted a broad array of the latest offerings.

"It will surely supplant silken gauze in lady's undergarments," the clerk commented... paused and then continued. "The fashion is now short, Mesdames and very full. Also... notice the fine color shades. Only the latest formulas and techniques in fabric dying are used and as you know they must precisely match the hues and tones of the outer garments. Mesdames will not find finer fashion anywhere in the world."

"Oh... look at this nightgown, Mimi," Anna exclaimed and then turning to the clerk asked, "What is it?"

"It is Maison Morin-Blossier, madam, of India foulard silk and fully trimmed with exquisite lace and hand-embroidered with the finest needlework of France. If I may offer my humble opinion, the vulgarities of machine embroidery have no place in the wardrobe of so elegant a young woman as you."

Anna smiled at the young man's style, but her attention was elsewhere and she exclaimed, "I love the way it flows, Mimi and the way the sleeves are trimmed and the wrist bands are gathered."

"Then you shall have it dear," Amanda said, motioning for the clerk to set the nightgown aside. "Your mother has allowed me to buy you one present and I should like this to be it."

"I love it, Mimi. Thank you so much."

"Will that be all, madam?" the clerk asked, quickly adding, "We have the finest petticoats... or perhaps silk stockings; we have the latest Pompadour designs... handkerchiefs in foulard or perhaps cambric, beautifully stitched."

"No thank you; this will suffice," Amanda responded assertively and the clerk nodded politely, content that he had fulfilled his obligation.

"Let's go down to Dennings, Mimi. I was at the spring opening and they had the most beautiful all-wool fabrics. You were looking for a street cloak weren't you...?"

"Remember we're meeting your mother at the museum, Anna; be keen to the time."

"Don't worry, Mimi. I want to show you the Brooklyn Bridge too."

"It's nearly four dear. Don't you think it's getting late? We can go another time," Amanda protested. Something was frightening her and she didn't want to go near the bridge. It was the kind of angst that has no apparent cause; it was just there lurking menacingly in the shadows of her mind.

"But we're almost there now, Mimi. I do want you to see it. We all went to the opening last Thursday, but we couldn't get near it there were so many people."

"No, dear. I must insist."

"Let's at least ride over it, Mimi."

It was late on the afternoon of Wednesday, May 30th, Decoration Day, and people were out and about all over the city, shopping, strolling and visiting the graves of loved ones. The weather was warm and the sky was clear. There was no hint of the horror that was about to happen. As their carriage swung under the elevated railroad on its approach to the bridge's Manhattan anchorage, the crowd cramming onto the pedestrian walk seemed unusually large and the bridge was packed for as far as they could see.

"We'll just ride over to Brooklyn and back on the carriageway, Mimi," Anna said. "You'll see how beautiful the harbor looks from high on the bridge."

As they approached the New York tower a woman's scream cut the air and a rush of people from the Brooklyn side forced their way through the arch and onto the stairs, trampling and crushing everyone in their path. Later a policeman stationed at the tower would testify that that one shrieking scream ignited the inferno. A frenzied panic followed as more and more people, believing the bridge to be collapsing, tried to squeeze through the narrow platform.

They could see thousands of people on the bridge behind the jam pushing relentlessly forward packing more and more bodies ever tighter into the bottleneck where the planked footpath passed around the central column of the tower and narrowed to access the stairs leading down to the anchorage promenade pavement. The throngs packing the walkway on the Brooklyn side, blocked by the tower and unable to see the devastation they were causing, drove forward like crazed cattle.

Hideous cries of agony filled the air and for a few seconds stunned everyone into inaction. Then from the carriageway they could see people dragged by the tremendous pressure of the mob against the iron railings and cables that enclosed the promenade, their clothes and flesh rented and ripped apart. Children were thrown down the steps and crushed as others thrashed and trampled them. Men and women were desperately trying to pull themselves up onto the railing, but were too weak to escape from the vicious and relentless vise. It was a cage of death. They watched a mother holding a little girl on her shoulders carried along helplessly until she reached the top of the stairs where she managed to push the child over the railing dropping her down onto the railroad tracks. There the girl clung to the iron lattice work only to watch her mother lose her footing and fall, her body trampled, scraped and dragged down the bloody steps.

Suddenly some men jumped from wagons on the carriageway and began pulling desperate victims over the railing onto the pavement, but it did little to loosen the crushing mass of flesh as more and more bodies jammed the narrow passage.

"You have to help these people," Amanda said to their driver as he tried to steady his nervous animals.

"I can't leave the horses, madam, they'll bolt for sure," the driver responded.

"Anna, we've got to do something," she turned frantically to her granddaughter.

"You stay here, Mimi," Anna ordered as she climbed down from the carriage and ran to the railing to do what she could. People were panicked and desperate to escape from the suffocating throng. Anna took hold of what ever she could reach and together with some others pulled as many as they could from the writhing mass of flesh.

For a time it seemed that nothing could control the surging crowd, driven by fear and determined to get off of the bridge. Finally the police, arriving in ever greater numbers, fought their way into the mindless horde with nightsticks swinging and slowly brought the madness to a halt.

At long last the clot was cleared and the two crowds were separated and forced to file slowly along opposite sides of the walkway. Proceeding past the platform of horror they had caused, they could clearly see their victims, battered and bloody, purple from asphyxiation, still heaped on the stairs and against the railings.

For Amanda, sitting in the carriage, it had all been a blur. She hardly noticed the fire and police wagons rushing to the scene and the chaotic struggle that followed. Even the unconscious young boy, badly broken and bruised, lying in her lap, disappeared forever from her memory. Later, all she would recall was the sight and scream of a frantic young woman holding an infant over her head and fighting to stay above the seething cauldron.

"We're taking him to the Chambers Street Hospital," Anna directed the driver. "Hurry, I fear he won't make it."

As they galloped down the carriageway toward Manhattan, Amanda's emotions were compressed inward by the sight of so many innocent people mangled beyond recognition, so many bodies lying loosely covered, like so much trash, by anything available, some crushed hats or a flattened parasol. Her nerves were raw.

She couldn't shake the thought that she had been directed by some higher power to see this, that she was destined to be here at this moment, forced to be helpless and suffer the utter emptiness of futility. Thoughts of her own death had lately made their appearance, prompted by her lost brother's plea for her to help him. She saw her own life reaching an end and wanted very much to believe that it had been meaningful and valuable, but she wasn't sure.

"What's wrong, Mimi?" Anna asked. "You're shaking; Are you alright?"

"I was thinking about Samuel. I'm frightened, Anna. This whole thing terrifies me beyond anything I've ever known and seems somehow connected to him."

Just after the war, many freedmen were wary of signing labor contracts for fear of being tricked back into bondage. Getting freedmen working in the fields in some semblance of slavery was for many of the South's better citizens the first priority and they tried to intimidate those who would act honorably with the former slaves. Many of the old guard just never could get used to free labor.

The war wasn't over a month before we saw the first apprentice law that bound Black children over to their old masters as apprentices, to protect them from idle or otherwise indigent parents who couldn't care for them, they claimed. Of course, knowing that they would not abandon their children, this was done simply to try to keep the parents from leaving the farms and was a kind of court sanctioned coercion.

The labor agents for Chinese coolies were all over the area too, but I never thought that was an answer. First you had to pay the man's passage from China and that was about three-hundred dollars. Then they wanted a five year contract at upwards of twenty dollars a month wages, deposited in a bank escrow account. That came to about fifteen-hundred dollars, up front. It was too much even if anybody had it.

Some tried share cropping. It had some advantages in dividing the risk of crop failures and pooling the investment costs, plus it gave the cropper greater incentive to bring in a big harvest. But, the land was dying and there just wasn't enough profit left to support two owners. It barely paid in good times and couldn't survive any drop in prices. It generally meant poverty everywhere they tried it.

Soon enough some planters were offering their land for rent at a fixed fee. Even though the rates were only about half that of share cropping it was more dependable for the landlord and freed him from any supervision or risk. It also offered the renter a chance to make a profit and ultimately buy his own land, which was what many Blacks wanted of course.

The better citizens, as they liked to think of themselves, were always afraid that the former slaves were going to rise up and massacre them. With so many free Blacks roaming around with no one controlling them they got more than a little nervous and began finding creative ways to throw anyone they thought might be dangerous into jail.

Then when the number of Black prisoners went way up somebody proposed the idea of convict leasing as a creative way to get compliant field hands. But, as you might imagine, there weren't nearly enough of them to even dent the labor shortage.

The former slaves put a lot of faith in the Yankees to help them. But, they never got much from the army or the Freedman's Bureau either for that matter. It quickly became apparent that the only answer was to control the state government, and that chance came when the so-called Republican Reconstruction took hold.

This, I think, was the first we saw of the KuKlux. They did some barn burning and the like to try to scare any planters who they thought were cooperating with the Yankee carpetbaggers or were part of the Loyal Leagues. For awhile the closest they came was up in Coahoma County up around Friar's Point. Then when the elections got close, we finally got our share. It was a very scary time.

These KuKluxers were loose gangs of men determined to keep law and order as they defined it. Mostly their purpose was to control the movement and activities, particularly political aspiration, of the Blacks and any Whites who threw in with them. They operated at night and in secret and used intimidation and threat mostly, but there were reports of severe beatings and even murders. They seemed most threatened by schools and burned many of them. An educated Negro, especially one with political ambition, was not to be tolerated...

...There was no way to tell man or beast. The hooded horses and riders, masked beneath flowing gowns of white, glided past like the ghosts they pretended to be. The horses were lathered and tired and it was evident that they had come many miles to do their grisly deed. Guns and swords were in plain view and, as if to make their intent unmistakable, a hangman's noose swung from every pummel.

It was the regular practice of the Ku Klux Klan to call their minions in from afar, beyond the county and even across the state-line if practical to ensure that no man or horse be recognized. This was particularly important if a murder was to be done.

They paused and dismounted at the top of a rise overlooking the planter's house. His sin was the schoolhouse built on his land and his disdain for the warning he had received to stop encouraging Negro equality. The leader stood high in his syrups and spoke.

"This is the windy night of the bloody moon. But, the lightning only slumbers in the serpent's cave. Make ready you ghouls of Confederate dead. Make ready for revenge on this White trash who clings to the black soulless beast."

Torches were lit and the hooves of their horses wrapped in heavy burlap to muffle their sound. They rode in a long line to give the appearance of being many more than they were, an almost silent, smoky blur, slowly circling around and around the house like thousands of dead ghosts risen up from their graves at midnight to exact revenge on all enemies of the South.

Gradually they wound themselves tight around the house, filling the front yard and blocking any avenue of escape.

"Men of grey arise! The hour has come to crawl from beneath the bloody dirt of your graves. The great Cyclops calls you to take revenge on this scalawag scum that's been found in Dixie's Land."

Inside the house the farmer prepared to defend himself. A week earlier he had found a note on his door written in blood and signed K.K.K. ordering him to leave the state within seven days, or die. The man refused to go saying he owned the land and would not be driven out. Besides, he warned his wife, they would only burn everything down if he left. The only answer was to fight.

"Come out you bastard or we'll come in there and get you."

"Stay back or I'll fire," the man answered.

"Fire if you will. We'll kill you anyway."

Suddenly the door collapsed inward under the thunderous blow of a heavy timber. It was only a feint, but it fooled the frightened farmer who let both barrels blast harmlessly through the dark empty doorway. The masked men rushed in behind it firing pistol rounds into the roof. The man drew his sword, backed into the corner and prepared to die fighting, when he saw his wife knocked to the floor and bleeding.

"You cowards," he yelled. "Let her go and I'll do what you say."

"Take him outside," the leader growled and the man was dragged into the front yard where his clothes were slashed from his body with knives in such frenzy as to leave his arms and back cut and bleeding.

"So you want to be a leader, you worthless turd. Well here's your death warrant; you can lead the way to hell," the man snarled handing a leather strap to one of the designated executioners.

The farmer was flogged mercilessly until his tormentor was exhausted beyond continuing. Several times he was pulled to his feet only to be beaten down again, kicked and stomped in the dirt and dust until he was little more than a bloody pulp.

His wife begged the men to stop, but they wouldn't listen. "Please, God have mercy," the woman screamed. "Let him die in peace. He surely can't live through this."

Boots rudely pushed and kicked the man over on his back. He was unrecognizable and barely breathing.

"Get him to his feet," the leader commanded. Several times they pulled the man up only to have him fall back, limp and unconscious, to the ground.

"Why, he's faking the possum. Let me shoot the son-of-a-bitch," a voice said.

"We don't need to waste a bullet on this piece of shit," the leader answered and with all of his weight twisted the heel of his boot down into the farmer's throat, crushing his windpipe and slowly killing him.

She shot straight up in the bed, soaked with sweat. "What is it, Mandy? Are you alright?"

"It was a horrible nightmare, Tom. I can't get over what we saw today. I don't think I'll ever get over it."

Thomas was worried about his wife. The undertaking to Mississippi was becoming increasingly problematic and he wasn't sure if they were up to it. "Can I get you something, Mandy, a cup of tea?"

"No, Tom. It was just the strain of today. I'm fine."

"I think we should take Anna with us, Mandy. She wants very much to come and I think we'd be better off if she were there to help."

"What do James and Melissa say?" Amanda responded. "Have you discussed it?"

"They have no objections and in fact they think it would be good for her to venture out a bit."

Amanda was relieved at the thought of having Anna with them. She loved and trusted her husband, but there were things she couldn't tell him, doubts and fears that she didn't want him to know about. "I think that would be wonderful, dear. I can't wait to tell her."

Chapter Nine

She couldn't sleep and lay quietly, waiting until the rising sun would let her return to Samuel's memoir. She was very still and careful not to wake Thomas. This would be the third time she had tried, each time searching for clues about who he really was and each time it made her nervous. The writing had a serious quality that belied the brother she remembered and she thought about how life surely changes us all. It was not yet dawn when she started reading, straining to see in the dim early morning light.

> *It wasn't long before we began hearing more and more about this KuKlux and how Mississippi was now a realm of the invisible empire and that there was going to be a meeting to elect a Grand Cyclops to head some kind of den nearby. They said that if we didn't join and do something fast the whole South would crumble. There were meetings every place that had an open whiskey bottle. I went to one, but I didn't say much, especially when it sounded like they were talking about me...*

"...The KuKlux is necessary to control the Blacks. They won't stay put; they abandon their contracts, and the uppity insolence of them is unbearable, especially as they get roused up by their leaders at these nighttime political meetings."

"You mean the "Loyal Leagues?"

"Yes, damn it, the damned loyal leagues. They're nothing but tools for the carpet bagging Yankee bastards and their scalawag toadies. It's the way the Republicans plan to ram it down our throats..."

> *...The whole thing with all of its Dragons and Titans and mumbo jumbo was intended to intimidate the freed man and scare him back into bondage by taking advantage of his superstitious nature. But, it seems like, with all of its secrecy and ritual it appealed to a lot of men who were just down and out and looking to belong somewhere. There were a lot of Johnnie Rebs back from the war just trying to latch on to something.*
>
> *I never agreed with this radical reconstruction. Why anyone would think that you could turn the whole political and social way of life in a place upside down overnight and not have trouble is still beyond me. But, that's exactly what they did...*

"Well it's nice to see that a big town like New York is finally fielding a team, not that you'll ever beat Boston," Thomas teased.

The Boston Beaneaters were in the city to begin the season series with the New York Gothams. Boston was the dominant team of the decade and highly favored to repeat as league champions. Nevertheless, James was confident that the fledgling home team, having acquired several premier players, was poised to pull an upset. Anna loved baseball and insisted on bringing her reluctant grandmother. Thomas promoted the idea thinking it might help to get Amanda's mind off of her troubles.

"What is there about this game that fascinates you so, Anna?" her grandmother asked.

"It's a very nearly perfect game, Mimi, a scientific game, requiring keen calculation and alertness at all times. It's just so interesting. I'll explain it all... you'll see."

The Gothams took the field and Anna began. "The aim of it is very elementary; simply send as many men as possible around the diamond and back to home plate."

"And each one counts as a point," Amanda interjected, "Your grandfather has already tried this."

"Correct, Mimi, each counts as a... run... as it is termed in baseball."

"Now you see it makes no sense already. Why would you call it a run when the player has stopped running. Why not just call it a point?"

"Yes, you could, but... well the first batter is coming up so let's go on. Each team has an equal opportunity to come in to bat. This is called an inning."

"Yes, I remember this. Your grandfather told me this. It refers to the fact that the team is in from the field." Amanda shook her head. "But what I don't understand is that only one of the teams is in; the other is still out."

Anna pushed on. "The batsman must hit the ball into fair territory, then drop the bat and run to first base. As soon as three batsmen have been put out, the team in the field comes in to bat. There are nine of these innings."

"Well, sometimes there are more than nine, aren't there dear?" Amanda asked, but before her granddaughter could respond the batter hit the ball.

"There, you see, Burdock has bounced it through into the outfield and has reached first base. Watch him now as the next batter comes up. He's going to try to steal second base if he can." Anna moved to the edge of her seat and Amanda could feel the excitement rise in her. "See the coacher there in the box next to him?" she said pointing.

The old woman strained to pick up the action that her granddaughter was describing.

"Now listen as the pitcher delivers his pitch."

"Go!"

"Did you hear him yell go to the runner?"

"Yes, but he didn't go."

"Correct, this was a feint, a false signal. The coacher really didn't want him to go."

"So he yells go when he doesn't want him to go?"

"Well... he yells go when he wants him to go too?"

"So he yells go when he wants him to go... and when he doesn't want him to go he also yells go?"

Anna could see through the corner of her eye that her grandfather was thoroughly amused by it all, but went on bravely. "He will yell go with a particular inflection of voice when he wants the runner to go, otherwise it's only a fake."

"Well that makes no sense, dear."

"Why not, Mimi? It's a way to disguise when the runner will try to steal."

"Then why yell anything at all, dear. Just keep quiet about it. That's what I'd do."

Anna had no idea what to say next and was saved by a question.

"Now this is something I don't understand. Why did the catcher move up right behind the batter? Isn't that very dangerous?"

"It is, yes, but the batter now has two strikes against him and a third strike must be caught by the catcher before the ball hits the ground. He can't stay ten feet back any longer. See how he crouches low to avoid being clubbed by the bat?"

"Go!"

"There he goes, finally." Amanda remarked.

"Ball three," the umpire barked. The catcher's throw was high and the runner slid under the tag.

"Safe," the umpire roared with his arms in the air running toward the play from his position a few feet up along the first base line.

Thomas now joined in. "If Burdock can reach third he will almost surely score. See him edging off the base? He has a very good lead. Watch for him to go on this next pitch."

Suddenly the shortstop broke for second base behind the runner and the pitcher without the slightest hint and seemingly by magic whirled around and threw a blazing ball to the base. Burdock slid low, but to no avail.

"You're out," the umpire yelled, raising his fist.

"Alright!" James burst out jumping to his feet and playfully patting his dejected father's shoulder. "What a throw, Anna, did you see that?"

Anna turned to her grandmother. "Now you see how that happened. The catcher sees the whole field and knew that the runner was too far off the base. He signaled the fielders to make that pick-off play and even though the pitcher was throwing blind he knew the shortstop would be there to catch the ball."

"Yes... it was very exciting dear; don't you think so, Tom?"

"Yes, dear," he replied with a smile, happy that the day out had, at least momentarily, lifted her spirits.

"The Pennsylvania Railroad terminal is in Jersey City, father," James said as their carriage approached the ferry at the foot of Debrosses Street. "You can't use Grand Central this time."

"That's just as well, James, believe me," Thomas retorted, although he was beginning to become concerned about the amount of luggage they had brought.

"This takes you across the Hudson to the depot. It's very easy; you're going to take the Pennsylvania Railroad to Nashville via Cincinnati. There you change to the Mississippi and Tennessee for Grenada via Grand Junction, Tennessee. So you're straight through to Nashville and then one change, and maybe not even that if the IC has bought or leased them all by then."

"The IC?" Thomas reacted with a squint.

"Illinois Central Railroad, father, the first of the great land grant bonanzas. They hit some tough times after the war, but now they're showing some sustained growth. I've been looking at railroads lately and the Illinois Central is very attractive."

"Are you thinking about common stock? Railroads look risky to me, always did. Too political, besides the country's getting tired of underhanded railroad practices."

"No, I don't think their stock is going up much. What they're doing is driving up the value of a lot of troubled southern lines that can't afford to rebuild after the war. It's a matter of figuring out what they'll go after next. We made some money last year when they leased the Chicago, St. Louis and New Orleans road."

"What happened to Standard Oil, you seemed very keen on that last Christmas?"

"I'm afraid to take the chance I guess. Hamrick and Son has always been in shipping. There's so much land in this country, so much potential farm product just waiting to be brought to market. Railroads are the future. The west is wide open."

It was their last day in the city and Thomas savored the short time he had with his only son. He let James pour out his plan. It reminded him of conversations he had had with his own father a half-century earlier. He knew the business had to grow and change with the times, that it wasn't schooners any more as it had been for his grandfather, nor was it canals and steamboats as it had been for him. Now it was more about railroads, investments and speculation.

Delmonico's restaurant filled the corner of Fifth Avenue and Fourteenth Street, stretching all the way to Broadway. The main dining room, walled with mirrors, silver chandeliers hanging from the frescoed ceiling, tables festooned with flowers and cut glass, faced Fifth Avenue, where many came daily to see and as many came to be seen. Private carriages parked two abreast filled half of Fourteenth Street.

"Take us around to the Broadway entrance," James instructed. "We'll eat in the men's café. That way we can have a good cigar." Smoking, drinking and eating lunch in the men's café was more to the taste of the city's commercial and industrial elite. There one heard very few requests for truffled grouse or oysters and Chablis.

The men's café was more austere than the main dining room, with marble floors and tabletops, but the air of elegance was unmistakable in the professionalism and competence of the French style wait staff. Delmonico's was expensive and that was precisely why many of them liked it. The menu was extensive and the cuisine was the most refined and celebrated in America, but, despite all of that, in the men's café at Delmonico's one heard but one word, steak.

"The portion for one, sir, is quite enough for two," the waiter cautioned, but James would have none of it.

"...and bring us a bottle of the house claret," he added, then turning to his father commented, "It's quite good. I was never one to overpay for fancy French wine."

"Why the Illinois Central?" Thomas asked knowing that his son wanted to tell him more.

"It was built on this transport dilemma. In a way so was Standard Oil. Producing is not the problem in this country. Moving the product, that's the problem. Rockefeller understood this and so do the railroad tycoons, men like Cornelius Vanderbilt. He saw it coming and divested from steamships to railroads and was one of the richest men in the world when he died. You've got to stay ahead of the times."

"And fill the pockets of the politicians, don't forget that," Thomas chided. "Those railroad fortunes were made on big giveaways of public lands!"

"The key to success was getting federal land grants, that's true and that was the goal of every Illinois politician before the war. At first they tried for preemption rights as an angle to get the government land. Getting a direct land grant was not considered likely because of so much opposition."

"I never liked land grants myself, James," his father went on. "It's a fairness issue it seems to me because everyone has a right to share in the benefits from government lands. Unfortunately, it was never about getting it only a question of who got it."

"Well, you're right, in a way that was the problem because they could never get the votes in Congress for direct land grants as long as it was seen as benefiting only Illinois. Then a slick Senator named Stephen Douglas figured it out. To get the votes he sweetened the pot to include lands in Mississippi and Alabama."

Thomas laughed, "Naturally, isn't that how it's always done. Make sure everybody's in on it. You talked about a pork barrel, now that's the real pork barrel."

"That's right, as long as everybody gets their piece of the pie. Of course there were objections that it was illegal because the Constitution doesn't allow for the building of a railroad, which they said the grant of lands was merely a disguised way of doing."

"That's funny," Thomas chuckled cynically. "Since when has the Constitution ever gotten in the way of making money?"

The beef was juicy and rare. The power of a Delmonico's steak to pause a conversation between men was truly amazing. Thomas didn't like his son's plan, but was resolved to say no more believing in the end it would only be resented. They finished their meal and the last of the wine.

"Garçon, bring us two Havana Cubanos," James called to the waiter. "They're rolling them right here in the city now." Then he leaned forward and added, "There was one thing I wanted to ask you father, since you're going to Mississippi. See what you can learn about what the IC might be up to between the Yazoo and the gulf."

CHAPTER TEN

Suddenly the slamming steel door jarred her senses and she looked up. They had been underway for almost an hour when the conductor appeared for their tickets. She scanned the long Pullman sleeping car for Thomas and Anna, but they were nowhere in sight.

"Tickets, madam and your berth reservations as well if you would please," the very proper official began. "My name is Charles," he continued as she sorted the papers out from among her things. "I am the Pullman conductor. I will handle everything. There will be no need for you to be bothered beyond this."

Again Amanda strained to see if Thomas and Anna were in the car as she handed him the documents. "I'm traveling with my husband and my granddaughter. I have their tickets too."

The conductor studiously examined the documents and then said, "Your party will be in this same car continuously from Jersey City to Nashville, Mrs. Hamrick. There will be a one-hour delay in Cincinnati at about 6 AM tomorrow to put on the Jim Crow cars, but that shouldn't interrupt your sleep."

"The Jim Crow cars?" Amanda reacted with a questioning frown.

"From Cincinnati we pass non-stop to points South and Tennessee requires segregated railroad cars, madam. All first class Negro passengers must change cars in Cincinnati."

Amanda said nothing. They both saw the impeccably dressed Black gentleman sitting alone in the alcove opposite them and the conductor felt it necessary to elaborate. "There are separate but equal accommodations made for them, madam. Both Pullman and the Pennsylvania Railroad regret this inconvenience, but it is now the law in Tennessee."

"Oh there you two are," Amanda reacted, interrupting. "The conductor has asked for our tickets, Tom. This is my husband, Thomas and my granddaughter, Anna."

"How do you do," the man said with a polite nod.

"Please go on, sir. I apologize for the interruption," Thomas said, noticing the man's apparent impatience.

The conductor continued. "You will arrive in Nashville at 7 AM tomorrow morning. There you will change trains. Your Pullman service continues in a palace parlor car on the Mississippi and Tennessee Railroad for the last leg of your journey. Be advised that there is a two hour wait in Nashville and I suggest that you plan to eat breakfast in the town. Your train departs at 9AM for Grenada, Mississippi via Grand Junction, Tennessee. You should reach your last stop at 1 PM."

"What about our things?" Thomas asked.

"Not to worry, sir. Your luggage will be forwarded. I suggest that when you reach Grenada you express your trunks and bags directly to your hotel."

"How does that work?" Thomas asked, somewhat reluctantly, not wanting to create any needless delay.

"When you reach your destination, the Pullman porter will assist you," was the terse reply as the conductor turned and continued down the car.

Thomas said nothing, although it was obvious that he was dissatisfied with the response. The Black man was watching and asked, "You were given a numbered brass token that corresponds to each piece of your luggage?"

"Yes."

"Just give those to the porter when you reach the end and tell him where you want it to be delivered."

"Well, I thank you, sir. I appreciate your help."

"Not at all, sir," the man responded. "And don't forget to add a little gratuity."

"Will that help?" Thomas said with a friendly chuckle. The two men shook hands and exchanged smiles before Thomas asked. "Would you care to join me for a smoke, sir?"

Amanda signaled her assent and the two men walked slowly through the car, steadying themselves on the seat corners as they went. "Please go back to your reading, Mimi," Anna said reaching for one of the many magazines left strewn about the car. "Don't let me disturb you; I love to look at the Harper's and Leslie's. The artists are so talented."

There's no doubt that the carpetbag governments in this state were a disaster and when they gradually lost the confidence of the Blacks, everyone knew they would collapse. The whole thing finally came to a head during the elections of 1875. The Democrats were determined to get back into power come hell or high water and many prominent Blacks, even Senator Revels, went over to their side.

Maybe it was all the racial trouble that ultimately led to it; I don't know. The bloody race riot in Clinton in September shook up a lot of people. Nobody really knows how it started, but when the dust cleared there were dead on both sides. The rumors were flying that the Blacks were gathering in the woods and planning to burn the place to the ground and hundreds of armed White men from all over the area rushed in to protect the town, mostly by murdering any Blacks they could find. It looked like race war for sure was about to break out. The carpetbag governor Ames made a plea for federal troops, but Grant said it was time for the South to take care of its own problems. This meant the end of reconstruction in Mississippi because after that things were sure to sort out the way the Whites wanted.

Ames didn't trust the militia so he armed Black companies to keep the peace and that only made things worse. He wanted to make a show of force, but the so-called best citizens could never abide the sight of Black men marching around with drums and bugles. For weeks it seemed like everybody was carrying some kind of weapon and the Whites had a lot more of them. Some of us went down to Jackson to try to talk some sense to Ames, but we didn't get far. He knew his days as governor were numbered.

Most Blacks were frightened and wanted no part of it so they steered clear of the polls that year. They got scared for sure; there was a lot of intimidation, killings and lynching around that time, but it was also a matter of being fed up with confrontation. They just wanted to work and improve themselves and that was never going to happen without peace and harmony between the races. Of course a lot of the old guard was still determined to get back to where they were before the war and that wasn't going to happen without more trouble.

So that's where we were at when the Democrats took back the state government after the election. They impeached and removed Ames and as many carpetbaggers as they could and undid just about every law that had been passed since the war. The scalawags kept their mouths shut and the Yankees cleared out of the state pretty fast after that, but I had no place to go...

..."What in tarnation happened over in Clinton?"

"I'm tellin' ya, Sam, the Republicans are schemin' it. They're gettin' desperate. They know the Blacks are scared to come out for 'em this time. A good race riot will get the federal troops in just in time to buck 'em up before the election. That's Ames' plan. Why else would he organize these damn confabs with the Democrats? It's a setup for a riot that's all it is."

"Well... I want to know?"

"They were having the usual political carryin's-on with pork do-ins an' all. One a them barbecue debates that Ames organized where the Republican makes a speech and they all cheer and then the other guy makes one and the Democrats cheer and then the two sides insult each other for a while."

"Well damn it... I want to know?"

"Well, Sam, I'll tell ya if'in ya give me a chance... I hear tell it was a powerful hot day. A couple thousand people were there, mostly Blacks, when somebody sparked it and guns went off. Three or four was killed on each side before everybody pull-footed out a there."

"Well... who started it, Cyrus?"

"What in hell's difference does it make? It was bound to happen sooner or later with this election comin' on like it is. The point is it's gotta be stopped before it's too late. There's a special train goin' down there from Grenada. I think we oughta go."

"And get ourselves killed?"

"Look, every hotheaded cracker in three counties is headin' there. I hear there's thousands a Black boys camped out in Jackson beggin' for guns to protect they're selves. They got their families hidin' in the woods and swamps. Ames don't know what to do. He's just backin' and fillin' and prayin'."

"What do you think we can do?"

"Talk sense to em'. He's bringin' in Gatlin' guns for God's sake..."

"What?"

"Gatlin' guns and wagons of munitions are coming up from Vicksburg. Them Black boys is mighty worried and mighty fed up, if they start shootin' them Gatlin' guns at the White boys they might never stop."

The sleeping car was laid out in a series of alcoves along the walls, each made up of two small couches facing each other. A small table placed between them served for dining. With the table removed the two couches could be lowered to become a bed, while a second berth overhead was created by lowering a ceiling panel. The whole bed chamber could then be enclosed by a heavy curtain. "These Pullman cars are quite the thing wouldn't you say?" Thomas commented, trying to start the conversation as they walked.

"When properly managed," the man answered, "and that's not always the case I'm sorry to say. It's a good bit of work taking care of one of these cars with all the conversions, keeping beds clean and sanitary, not to mention the water closets. I've traveled on some less than satisfactory trains."

There were three other Pullman cars, a buffet dining car and two parlor cars with the most luxurious upholstered swiveling chairs. The first parlor was well occupied with nearly all the seats filled and they continued through the dining car. Thomas sensed the incongruous clash between the calm serenity of spotless white table cloths and flowers and the people sipping their coffee and tea in perfect comfort with the screaming mass of steam and steel that they really were. "It's amazing to me how steady this train is. We must be going fifty miles an hour."

"These Pullman cars are very well balanced and ballasted," the man answered turning his head back briefly as they passed into the second parlor. This one however was empty. "This is my private car," the man said. "We can relax and have our smoke right here."

Thomas was a bit puzzled by the man's remark. "I don't believe I learned your name, sir."

"Amos Powell," the man replied and offered his hand. Thomas told the man his name and took two cigars from his jacket pocket, but Powell protested with a smile and reaching into his vest produced a cigarette box. "Please, Mr. Hamrick, try one of mine."

"Cigarettes, Mr. Powell? I've never tried one."

"These are top of the line. I got away from cigars, too busy. Cigarettes are much more convenient and very satisfying. Try one; you'll see."

Thomas took the cigarette, "Richmond Straight Cut," he read musingly from the package. "I'll remember that."

"Just be sure they're genuine number one Allen and Ginter. They're the best."

Each seemed at ease with his new acquaintance and the two men sat back in comfort to smoke.

"You seem to be a man who travels regularly, Mr. Powell. As you are a Black man, this Jim Crow business must be a bit vexing for you."

"Well... if I let it I suppose it would be, but I learned a long time ago not to be bothered by such things and especially while traveling. There are enough unforeseen difficulties and discomforts in life. Those that we understand and can anticipate should be the least of our worries."

"That's very admirable of you. Are others of your race so inclined?"

Powell avoided answering by asking a question of his own. "I gather you're not a traveling man, Mr. Hamrick."

Thomas, too, parried with a question. "Why did you call this your private car, Mr. Powell?"

"The Pennsylvania Railroad provides me with my own first class Pullman car. That way I don't need to be concerned with Mr. Crow. So in answer to your earlier question... I guess I'm not the right Black man to ask."

Thomas was intrigued by this well spoken and wealthy Negro and was compelled to find out more about him. "You must be a very important man, Mr. Powell. What kind of business are you in?"

"I'm a merchant, Mr. Hamrick. I buy and sell coal, much of which is shipped on this railroad I might add, which is why I get special consideration."

"And you obviously are a very successful merchant as well, congratulations."

"I'm fortunate, Hamrick, that's all. My grandfather was a slave who worked Sundays in a coal mine to earn his freedom. Then my father started peddling coal. He carried it himself to the towns around the mine in a donkey cart and saved his money. Now his son doesn't dig and he doesn't carry. He brokers coal shipments across six states from behind a desk. I'm a fortunate man, Mr. Hamrick, but not so foolish as to think I did it myself. It takes generations for a people to rise in societal status. The children should have greater opportunities than their parents, that's all. We stand on the shoulders of our forefathers."

Thomas understood the man well. He knew that his own wealth and social standing was the result of inherited wealth. It was a leg up which he enjoyed that not everyone had. As a Black man this same sense of unworthiness had recently insinuated itself into the conscience of Amos Powell. The economic plight of the freed slave carried with it an element of guilt for him and he wanted to relieve it.

Powel broke his concentration. "Have you ever heard of a school called the Hampton Institute?"

Thomas said no with his expression and the man went on. "It's a Negro school down in Virginia trying to train teachers. But, this school also stresses work and the mastery of manual skills, especially farming so people can earn a living. The head, the heart and the hands, that's their motto."

"And what is your association with this school, if I might ask?"

"Well, another school like it is starting up in Alabama at a place called Tuskegee and they need money. I'm going down there to see what I can do for them."

"You may be right, Powell. Higher education could be the key to Negro advancement."

"Every Black person in this country believes that education is the route to success, Hamrick, but none of them have a real answer to exactly how knowing Greek or reciting Shakespeare, is supposed to put food on the table. The Negro people in the South are barely able to avoid starvation and cannot be helped by abstract education. They need skills that they can sell now. That's why this kind of school, industrial training type of schools, like Hampton and Tuskegee, are what's needed." Powell went on cynically, gesturing with his chin toward the Negro Pullman porter passing through the car. "See that man there? He probably has a college education."

Thomas sensed an undercurrent of anger in Powell, but was not sure exactly what was causing it. "Tell me more about this Tuskegee school," he said, sidestepping the issue.

"I met a most persuasive woman from there, one Olivia Davidson, who so impressed me with the earnestness of their efforts that I determined to go and see for myself. Apparently they've bought some land, an old rundown plantation, some shacks. Everything needs renovation and they have no money. I'm told that the students themselves are putting up the buildings for their own school. I was struck by the worthiness of this and I hope I can help them. I really want them to succeed if for no other reason than to show that we can lift ourselves up."

"It sounds like a marvelous cause, Powell. But, why do you feel it necessary to go down there yourself?"

"Well there are those who say it's not enough, that it's just an accommodation that will only lead to perpetual second class citizenship for Blacks. But, nobody says it should stop with learning a trade. That's the start. I think it's economic equality that comes first, don't you, and then comes social equality? What did they get by chasing political power in the South? They got nothing in the end and will get nothing but Jim Crow. Well meaning Whites are getting tired of worrying about the Negroes. It's time for us to worry about ourselves... But, that's enough about me, Hamrick. What about you? Is it business or pleasure as they say?"

"We're going down to Grenada, Mississippi. It seems that my wife's brother left her a cotton plantation along the Yalobusha River just east of there."

"A valuable one I hope?"

"Apparently not," Thomas responded. "Or at least according to the lawyer it's next to worthless and I guess there's some liens or something on it too. Anyway, my wife wants to see it before she decides what to do."

Powel nodded. "Most of the bottoms in Mississippi have been under cultivation for a long time and are pretty much worn out from what I here. Not to mention the war and the neglect that much of that land has suffered since."

"Do you do any business with the Illinois Central Railroad?" Thomas asked remembering his promise to James.

"Some."

"The reason I ask is that my son seems to believe it to be a good investment. What do you say?"

"The shipping rates are very competitive between the lines and the margins are not great. The real money is always made in land speculation, Hamrick. These big railroads, especially that one, are all about cashing in on the rise in real-estate prices. That's why they're always looking to lay new track."

"I think he understands that and he's watching their recent expansion into the South."

"But..." Powell went on with a sly smile, "you've got to know where they're going and how they're planning to get there."

"Yes, exactly."

"I'll tell you one thing. There's a lot of money still to be made in Mississippi, in the Yazoo bottoms and even in the northeast uplands; I wish him luck."

Chapter Eleven

The dim glow of the distant gas light sent shadows shimmering along the drawn curtains. Anna had already climbed into the upper berth and the old couple was lying awake in the lower. The swaying rumble of the car was beginning to work its hypnotic spell on Thomas when the conductor's voice boomed through the darkened space. "As the porter must pay for lost or pilfered towels, I insist that the passengers refrain from appropriating them for personal use."

"You didn't pilfer a towel, did you Mandy?" Thomas, half asleep, joked innocently, but the topic triggered an angry response.

"How could I, Tom? I haven't been in there yet," she snapped leaning out of the berth to look back at the lady's room door. It had been continuously occupied for nearly two hours, but finally, at least now, no one was waiting. "One would think that they would be more considerate. A young woman was in there for nearly a half-hour!"

"The men's facility is free. Would you like me to ask...?"

"It's just not done, Tom, no," she bit back clearly very irritated. And then added sarcastically, "But then the men's toilet is always free isn't it?"

"You'd best get back there now before someone else gets ahead of you," Thomas suggested and Amanda agreed. Sitting up to straighten her robe she called up to her granddaughter in a loud whisper. "Anna do you need to use the convenience...? Anna..."

"She's sound asleep, I'm sure," Thomas said and his wife nodded as she left the privacy of the concealing curtains.

Thomas opened the crack far enough to watch her walk slowly away, steadying each step by grasping the sides of the upper berths. There was something too common and casual about the sleeping car after dark with all manner of humanity mixed together he thought and that made him fearful and protective. He watched her enter the toilet and didn't take his eyes off of the door until she reemerged.

"I demand to see the diagram," an angry voice behind him assailed the porter who was making up an upper berth. "I was not assigned an upper and particularly not one over the wheels."

"Yess sur," the porter slurred his response politely while continuing his task. Unlike the conductor, his income was decidedly dependent upon tips and what extra he could make fixing problems for passengers, doing errands or shining shoes at night. It wasn't beyond his talent to contrive a crisis or two to solve. "Dey be some sections open, sur. Yo' jus leave it ta me. I be takin' care of it for yo'."

Half-listening while waiting for his wife, Thomas once again went over what he was sure of. They had reservations at the Planter's Hotel in Grenada and had telegrammed the lawyer, Graham Fly. Everything that was controllable had been attended to; the rest was in the stars. He took the lawyer's reply from his pocket and read it again.

Have informed all parties STOP Will meet your arrival.

It was raining when they reached the Planter's Hotel. Graham Fly had decided to wait for them in the lobby. He informed them that the will was being contested by a man who claimed to be the rightful owner of the property. "It seems that one Jean Gareau had a partnership agreement with your brother when they unofficially combined their land in 1832. This contract held that should one die the partner would get a first option to buy out the other's half at the fair market value, to be determined by the Mississippi Valuation and Debt Law."

"Can we speak with this man?"

"We can't find him, madam," Fly responded before continuing. "But that's not important now because Gareau then sold his land as well as this option to a local man named Dinkin Sanford who is now exercising it. As I explained in my letter, Mrs. Hamrick, the document, which was witnessed by the sheriff, is a legal and enforceable contract that precedes the will."

"Is there any way to successfully contest this contract?"

"I don't believe so, Mrs. Hamrick. If you were his widow and not his sister, Mississippi law would likely protect your interests. Or if you were living on the plantation and were dependent upon it perhaps the court would grant you standing and hear a plea to break the contract, but since neither of these is the case, I'm afraid there's very little chance. Besides, what interest could you have in an almost worthless worn-out farm so far away from your home?"

Amanda didn't answer the question directly, but continued to pursue her purpose. "What would it take to make the plantation profitable?"

The lawyer exhaled disdainfully with a sigh and said slowly shaking his head, "cotton can be mighty fickle, Mrs. Hamrick. She'll promise you more and give you less than any other thing that grows. You don't want to even dream about trying to keep that old place going. She won't share-crop that's for sure and renting won't be worth your while either."

"What if it were undertaken modestly using only the best fields and methods? Would it do to support the people who are living there now?"

"First of all, it doesn't matter if you're planting ten acres or ten thousand the problem is always the same. It takes two men to harvest what one man can grow. Now with all the Blacks here about renting or sharing you won't find the pickers to bring in even a small crop. That's if you even get one."

"But what about the people still living there? Surely they know what to do."

"They could probably muddle through, but where would that get you. The way the market is it takes a damn near perfect year to make a profit. Either you get too much rain so you're constantly chopping grass and weeds or not enough and the plants die of drought."

Amanda began to protest, but Fly politely raised his hand to prevent her and pushed on. "Please, Mrs. Hamrick, let me tell you more. First there's cut worms to get those first little shoots and if they get up alive then there are the lice and caterpillars. If you get through that and start to see some fruit, the boll worm will be waiting for it too."

And before she could fully comprehend this barrage the man struck again. "Now, did I mention wilt and rust and leaf blight... And while you're sweating through all of this you'll be seeing the market price slipping lower and lower. Why it's the bane of southern agriculture, madam and true what they say: cotton brings almost nothing because almost everybody brings cotton?"

At this point Thomas interrupted, "I think Mr. Fly is right, Amanda," and then turning to the lawyer asked, "This man, Dinkin Sanford, is he prepared to purchase the place immediately?"

"Yes, I believe so. I have taken the liberty of scheduling a meeting this afternoon with Sanford and his attorney. This can all be taken care of today."

"No," Amanda interrupted forcefully, feeling rushed and not ready. "I want to walk on this land and talk to the people there first." She then turned to Thomas, "I need to see where my brother lived and find out who he was, Tom. I need to know that I'm doing the right thing."

Thomas nodded and turned to the lawyer, "How would we get out to the plantation, Mr. Fly?"

The lawyer, visibly annoyed at the delay, but convinced that Amanda would not cooperate until she was satisfied, offered his best advice. "There's a livery service, but that farm's at least fifteen miles out. It'll be expensive and I don't know if they'll even take you. You could rent gait horses or a horse and buggy. But, it's too long a ride for you folks and besides I wouldn't advise that you go alone."

"Where do we find the livery barn?" Thomas began, but before he had finished Fly offered an alternative.

"Olmstead had a wagoner named Henry. Uncle Henry they call him. He's been working a two mule hitch here about of late. I think he's trucking barrel staves over in old Tulahoma. He'll be your best bet."

"Where do we find this Uncle Henry?"

"I'll send him here to your hotel in the morning. Be ready to go first thing. Dress comfortably and bring something to eat. It'll be a good eight hours in that old wagon of his."

Uncle Henry was a short man, not much over five feet. His body was worn from a lifetime of work, but his spirit was strong and his eyes could still sparkle. It was mid-morning; the sun was already high and hot and to Amanda he seemed unnaturally layered in clothing for what was promising to be a very warm day, as though he were literally wearing everything he owned, she thought.

Patched pants bunched tight at his waist by a length of sisal were too big and loose, the baggy legs stuffed into woolen stockings were almost comical. His shoes were old black Brogans probably left from the war and on their third or fourth sole. A soft clean white cotton shirt neatly buttoned to the neck screamed satirically at the wrinkled collar and torn vest pocket. A tattered and dusty double-breasted canvas coat covered his superfluous suspenders.

"Your name is Uncle Henry I was told and that you might be hired to carry us to the Olmstead plantation. Do you know where that is?"

He took off his wide rimmed straw hat and smiled. "Yessum I knows jus' whare tis. Jus' down da big road a piece."

"Can you take us there?"

"Yessum, sho nuf can."

"Today?"

"Got no hosses... jus' mools... walkin' mools. Dey neber done much carriage work, sometimes dey pulled de surrey... but moesly nuffin' but pullin' wagons."

"That'll be fine, Uncle Henry. My name is Amanda Hamrick. I was Mr. Olmstead's sister. This is my husband, Thomas, and our granddaughter, Anna." Only Uncle Henry noticed the disapproving stares from passersby when Thomas stepped into the street to shake the Black man's hand. Uncle Henry nodded politely, but said nothing.

It was an old unpainted oak wagon of no particular pedigree, battered and worn, but, like its driver, not yet broken. It wasn't much more than a big box on wheels. The front seat had long since been discarded to make room for more cargo and Uncle Henry was accustomed to sitting on whatever was handy. He did however carry four heavy boards which when not used to heighten the sides could be fitted crossways to form benches that to Amanda seemed very high and ominous.

The old man nodded knowingly, climbing down from his perch. "Best be movin.' Like ta get dere befo' night fall."

He didn't like to admit it, but even Uncle Henry had made concessions to his advancing years and, no longer able to easily hoist himself up by stepping on the wheel hubs or even using the front step, he had added cross cleats to two of these planks and used them to make a wide and stable ramp to climb aboard from the back. Anna put the lunch basket and a small suitcase with a few things into the wagon and helped her grandparents up.

Thomas and Amanda watched curiously as before climbing in himself, Uncle Henry walked around to the pair of molly mules, scratched their ears and said something softly to each one.

"Do you mind if I sit up here with you, Uncle Henry?" Amanda said hoping to learn more about her perplexing new surroundings. "Those are very handsome mules, Uncle," she continued after a brief pause and drew a warm response.

"Deeze here be the sweetest pair a mools dere is."

She took an immediate liking to the wagoner seeing a genuine gentleman beneath the tattered façade and continued to try to seed the conversation. "Do you like them better than horses, Uncle?"

"A mool ain't like no hoss. You watch dem ears, dere always pointin' ta trouble. A mool doan take no chances wid nuffin'. Dat's why I likes 'em. Dey be careful. I seed lots a trouble in my days. Doan wan' no mo' trouble."

They made an interesting sight for curious onlookers as they rolled slowly through the town and Amanda waited until they were alone on the empty road before pressing on. "I understand that you worked for Mr. Olmstead before he died."

"Yessum, an' befo' dat, in de slave time I belong ta de Marsa Sam."

"What can you tell us about him, Uncle? What was he like then?"

Thomas leaned forward to listen as the old man continued. "Marsa Sam only hab 'bout forty, fifty slaves. He neber hab no need to look uppity and all de cullud folks say he be a kine man. Neber laid on de lash dat I eber seed."

"What kind of work did you do, Uncle, during slave times I mean?"

"I chopped cawten and cawn in da fiels jus like eberbody else and eben befo' da wah was ober, when dem Yankee sojers come, the marsa toll us, you be free."

"You must have been very happy, Uncle."

"Lord, mistus, I doan know what ta do wid myself. I roamed 'roun' an' 'roun' ebbry night, visitin' cawn cribs and tater kilns till I realize dat effin I starve it ain't nuffin' ta nobody. I gots ta worry bout my own self. So I got me behine a mool and neber paid dat freedom stuff no mo mine. Yo' know what da frog say when da pon's gettin' dry, mistus,?... Little bit's beta den nuffin'."

"So you came back to work for Mr. Olmstead?"

"Dey toll us we be free... den quick as lightnin' dem Yankee sojers dey wuz roundin' up all us darkies. Dey toll us we's vagrans an better getta contrak mighty quick or we be marchin' south. Marsa Sam gib me fi dollar a month. I nebber seed no money like dat befo. Den all de vagrans dey started comin' back ta da marsa and da Yankee sojers dey wuz the new pater rollers. Ole Marsa Sam done real good in doz times wid da Yankee sojers all 'roun'."

"That was some time before the war ended wasn't it?"

"Yessum, ole butcher Grant, dats what dey calls 'em 'roun here, he come right on down de Azoo right up ta de doe. De marsa be gone so when I seed dem Yankees comin' I hid the mools down in da holla. Marsa didn' hab no hosses by den wit de wah en all. Dem sojers dey tuk ebryting, broke down de smokehouse doe, ate all da hawg meat, dumped all da lasses an' milk on da groun', tuk all da cawn flour an' sugar. Dey eben kotched all da chickens and tuk 'em. Den dey wuz fixin' ta burn down de gin an' de big house when dey seed de mistess was Black."

"Your mistress was a colored woman?" Amanda reacted trying to subdue her sudden shock. This possibility had never occurred to her and it immediately complicated as much as it explained.

"Yessum."

"Mr. Olmstead was married to a Negress?" she repeated with deliberate emphasis, momentarily at a loss for how to continue, turning back toward her husband to be sure he heard.

"Yessum. Da White gentlemens herebout nebber were 'buv chasin' de fancy collud gals, ceppin ole marsa was in lub wid Sister Mattie. I knows it cause I hear'd em talkin' an moonin'."

The wagon rolled along in silence for two more hours and then suddenly they stopped for no apparent reason. "What's wrong Uncle?" Thomas asked.

"We got 'bout fo mo mile ta go and deez old gals be sayin' dey's tired. Dey won' go no wares till dey be good an' ready."

They stretched a bit, but barely had time to eat some fruit and figs before Uncle Henry called them back. "Bess be movin'."

The road ahead was a dark and gloomy tunnel, overhung by heavy willows and swamp oaks dripping with Spanish moss and the old man seemed nervous. "Nuffin 'tween here and dere ceppin but bad water and skeeters. Doe wanna be kotched in da tick woods and swamp afta dark."

Amanda couldn't contain herself any longer. "Tell us more about Mattie, Uncle. Was she legally married to Mr. Olmstead? Did they have any children? Where is she now?"

"Oh yessum, dey wuz legally married one time, but nowadays tings be difrent."

"Tell us the story, Uncle."

"Well, bess as I can recollect dey be livin' tagether fo' a long time. Dey hab one chile. Den wen de wah be ober de new laws say a man cain't live wid a woman ceppin he marries her. Call dat some kine a conkubinin an it ain't gonna be no mo. Now moesa deez conkubinas dey be cullud gals an so de new law say dey can marry dere White gentlemens."

"So after the war Mr. Olmstead married the woman he had lived with for many years."

"Dat's right mistus. Lan sakes dat cause a mighty big ta do. Dem White folks dey wuz all fer da conkubinen way caus dey say it tuk da steam outa de young White boys and kep em away from the poppa ladies."

"You said they had a child."

"He be bornd befo dat, but de new law say he be a true son a de marsa iffen dey jumps de broom. But dat's all changed agin. De Yankees be gone, an de times be difrent now."

"He's referring to the new laws since the end of the reconstruction," Thomas offered and then asked, "Is the marriage still legal today?"

"Nosuh, shor nuf ain't. De lahw now say White and Black cain't be tagether no mo, lessun it be in de chain gang. Mattie be mighty skaart wid de lynchin' en all."

"Where are they now Uncle Henry? Can we find them?"

"Dey be hidin' maybe."

"Surely someone on the plantation will know where to find them?"

"Harly nobody dere no mo. Some be squattin' in de quarters of a bandoned plantashun upland a ways... plowin' deir gardens en tato patches round deir an' stayin' quiet like. Iffin you starve hit ain't nuffin' t' nobody herebouts."

"Will you take us to this place, Uncle?"

"Yessum."

Chapter Twelve

Two huge weeping willows that draped over a wide colonnaded veranda, wrapping the two-story house on three sides, offered at once both a sense of secrecy and an unusually welcoming warmth. The main building itself was almost square with a shallow hip roof that formed a low truncated pyramid. A parapet enclosed a deck on the high flat roof from which, through the tall magnolias, the cotton fields could be seen stretching away into the distance. Together with the nearby stable of the same roof design and its cupola that in slave time served as a belfry, they gave an impression of ordered efficiency. It was a substantial but measured house showing signs of recent neglect, reflective of a gentleman of respectable estate, but declining means.

The front door opened into a long hallway reaching straight through to the back, which cut the house in half and led directly to a detached kitchen. A fragrant breeze flowing into their faces carried the delicious scent of something cooking and Uncle Henry hurried ahead to find the housekeeper.

"Aunt Lula be takin' care o' de big house now dat da boss be gone. She be in da kitchen I bliev."

Anna stayed behind on the veranda. There was no feature of southern architecture that spoke more of this lifestyle. It was indispensable to comfortable living in a climate that required coping with both a blazing sun and torrential rains. She sat down in the loveseat swing, looked at the lounging chairs and the dining table and fantasized about literally living outdoors, entertaining, greeting guests, eating lavish meals and, although she had never in her life tasted bourbon whiskey, she could see herself sipping mint juleps under the sweeping roof.

While they waited for Uncle Henry to return, Amanda looked from the hallway into the first room on the right. It was the formal parlor. Her eye quickly swept the room judging every detail by the magic of feminine instinct. The furnishings had the look of practicality and use. They were solid and durable without any hint of flare or ostentation. Yet even though it was plain, almost austere in fact, with no nick-knacks or trinkets to adorn the corner tables and mantles, the easy chair by the fireplace looked soft and inviting. Everything was common-place, but comfortable. It was a house that had been lived in, her intuition told her, and where happy children had omce played without fear of smashing some fragile nothing.

Angry animated voices from the back broke her concentration, but she couldn't make out any meaning in the jumbled sounds. She glanced into the business room across the hall on the left. Ledgers and correspondence still covered the big desk.

"Better to wait until everybody knows who we are," Thomas cautioned, sensing that his wife was eager to enter and explore the leftovers of her brother's shrouded life.

"Go get Anna," Amanda said suddenly a bit apprehensive and not knowing why.

Without warning, in the dying daylight, something white streamed ghostlike across the front yard directly toward the veranda steps. Anna felt her heart pound. She stayed still, pushed quietly back in the seat as it came closer, trying not to move or make a sound, straining to make out what it might be. Its shapeless milky mass floating free like a cloud came right up to her and suddenly stopped.

"Is that you?" a voice came from somewhere behind it and then a hand pulled the snowy stuff down and a face appeared. "Where's Lula? Who are you?"

For a few seconds Anna couldn't respond as relieved as she was that the ghost turned out to be very pretty girl of about her own age. Then her words came in a staccato torrent. "She's in the house with my grandparents. My grandmother was Mr. Olmstead's sister. My name is Anna Hamrick," she said shakily, while standing and extending her hand.

The girl struggled to get hold of the pile of white with one arm while reaching out with the other. "My name is Angeline Havens," she said and then asked apprehensively, "Are they talking about the plantation?"

"Yes, I think so. My grandmother has inherited it?"

"I guess I'd better come back then," she added softly and a bit sadly and Anna asked what it was she was carrying.

"My wedding dress," Angeline answered with a smile. "I was just bringing it from Aunt Effie to show Lula. It was her wedding dress before and she gave it to me. Aunt Effie's fixing it over and fitting it and such and I wanted to show her how well it fits and how proud she's going to be of it."

"Oh let me see it!" Anna reacted so spontaneously and honestly and with such genuine excitement that it immediately disarmed the young bride to be.

Angeline lovingly laid the exquisitely draped gown of white satin merveilleux down across the padded back of the swing. It wasn't the most expensive material, but it had a simple elegance and on such a beautiful bride, with the addition of petticoats and a train, it would be stunning.

"It's a splendid dress; I love the elegant high neckline," Anna said and Angeline gushed that it wasn't done.

"Aunt Effie won't do the beading on the bodice and sleeves until its properly fitted and that's what I came to show her."

"I'm sure she'll love it," Anna said and Angeline continued as though the two girls were old friends.

"I really hope she does; I really do. She always dreamed about a big wedding with bridesmaids and groomsmen. She wanted to have a wedding like those all the White folks had. Not a jump the broom wedding like the ones the slaves got. He went all the way to New Orleans to buy her this dress and the fancy French Chantilly lace for the veil; but she never got to use it. Now she wants me to wear it. She wants me to have the wedding that she dreamed about."

This kind of easy immediate intimacy was natural at their age and they each wanted to go on talking when Anna turned toward a voice from the doorway around the corner.

"Anna... Anna, are you there?"

"Here I am Bumpa, there's someone..." she began turning back, but the pretty Black girl with the wedding dress was gone.

"Dis here be Lula." Then he said for a second time and rather deliberately, "She be takin' care o' de big house now dat de boss be gone."

A tall graceful grey haired mulatto woman of about sixty emerged from the shadowed hallway. She had a smooth olive brown complexion and striking green eyes that hinted of some mysterious multiracial heritage.

"Hello, Lula," Amanda began cautiously. The woman reached out to shake Amanda's hand, looked her in the eye suspiciously, but at first said nothing. "I am Samuel Olmstead's sister. My name is Amanda Hamrick and this is my husband, Thomas and our granddaughter, Anna."

Thomas smiled, nodded and added, "My wife has inherited this plantation from her brother and we're here to see it and decide what to do with it. We were hoping that you and Uncle Henry and the others here could help us to find his son. Samuel told us that he wants this all to go to him."

"Yes, I know," the woman responded distinctly and in flawless English that surprised the old couple. "Uncle Henry told me who you were. You must be tired and hungry after coming all this way. Please come in; we have plenty."

"I wants yo' all te know," Uncle Henry said softening the scene, "dat Mistus Mattie-Lou be de bestus cook eber..." Then he tagged looking at Lula with a mischievous smile, "afta Granny Mo, dat is."

Amanda saw Uncle Henry's smile collapse and his countenance drop, but she didn't turn quickly enough to catch the venom that had flashed across Lula's face.

When they reached the kitchen, several choice pieces of chicken were already fried and stacked on a big platter staying warm on the side of the big black stove. Just the right amount of the lard was still hot in the heavy cast iron pan and Lula quickly began frying the grits.

"We could smell that chicken as soon as we reached the veranda, Lula," Amanda said, "I'm sure it will be delicious."

"Help yourself, Henry," Lula said, ignoring Amanda's remark and the old man put several pieces on a plate and started out the back door.

"Aren't you going to stay and eat with us?" Thomas asked.

"Bes' be seein' ta da mools," the old man answered nervously.

"Oh please stay, Uncle Henry?" Amanda added.

"Doan wanna be kotched out afta dark," he answered.

"Do you believe in ghosts, Uncle Henry?" Amanda innocently teased, encouraging the affable old man to continue the conversation.

"One time I wuz comin' down dis here road and lord I got dis jumpy feelin' dat dere was sumptin coming up behin' me... comin' up slow an' sneaky like. I's too scared to look ober ma shoulder, but den I hear'd it whooshin' an' I know'd it be de moonack an he be comin' fer me."

"What did you do, Uncle?"

"I run jez as fas as I do till I get ta de crick. De moonack he doan like ta cross movin' water, but I didn' stop, no sa. I run an holler all de way home and shut de doe."

"What is the moonack, Uncle Henry?"

"De moonack be a speerit what lives in de dark woods an' hides in de holla trees. Nobody eber seed de moonack and lived ta tell 'bout it."

"So the moonack isn't a ghost?"

Uncle Henry could have gone on longer, but at that moment he caught the glare in Lula's eye. "No, de moonack ain't no ghos," he said reaching for his plate of chicken. "I seed plenty a ghosses, talk to 'em eben." Only a few words later he was through the door and gone. "No, mistus, de moonack sure ain't no ghos."

Soon enough the hominy was piled on the plates beside the chicken. Some flour, a little seasoning and a bit of heavy cream stirred into the pan drippings made a simple, but satisfying, gravy that was poured over it all. They never ate a better meal.

"I wish Uncle Henry had stayed," Amanda began again. "He's very friendly. Don't you think so, Tom?" she added trying to engage the woman somehow in conversation.

"Yes," Thomas responded nodding absently, more concerned with chewing on his crispy chicken leg and then went on mindlessly, "He's afraid of ghosts I guess."

Amanda cringed thinking the comment would be off-putting, but Lula responded unexpectedly. "They all talk about ghosts all the time. As soon as it gets dark they think about ghosts. They tell their children ghost stories from the time they're babies. It's no wonder he's afraid of the dark."

"I take it you don't believe in ghosts, Lula," Thomas said politely extending the small talk for no apparent reason while reaching for another piece of chicken.

"There are no ghosts, Mr. Hamrick, or at least I have never seen one and never expect to I might add."

"Have you lived here for a long time?" Amanda redirected the conversation more precisely to the point.

"Yes... a long time."

"You must have known my brother very well."

"Yes... very well."

"I hope you'll help us, Lula. We need to speak to his wife and especially his son. Do you know where they are?"

"They're frightened. It's dangerous for Black people here, Mrs. Hamrick, especially educated ones."

"Is it the Ku Klux Klan that they're afraid of?"

Lula laughed shaking her head almost disdainfully and said, "Since the so-called redemption there's no more need for masquerading. But the same men are still here and they haven't changed. They'll never allow him to get this land... some worthless land maybe, but not this land. They'll kill us all first."

"Can't we rely on the authorities?" Thomas asked. "We've spoken to the lawyer, Graham Fly, in Grenada and he assures us that..."

"Graham Fly is a White man, Mr. Hamrick. Samuel's son is Black."

"But surely there has to be more to it than that."

"No... there doesn't have to be, Mr. Hamrick," she answered in a biting tone. "They want this plantation because they believe there's money to be made. And they mean to get it."

"Where can we find his wife and son?" Amanda asked again.

"Just give them what they want," Lula responded, ignoring the question, "and go back home."

"No," Amanda answered assertively. "I can't do that. I must carry out my brother's wishes."

"Your brother wished for a lot of things that he never got," Lula responded and then she turned to look Amanda in the eye and said, "Samuel was a good man, Mrs. Hamrick and he tried hard, really hard, but there was no way it was ever going to work, not here, not yet."

"You're talking about his marriage to a Black woman?" Amanda asked rhetorically.

"They were people, Mrs. Hamrick, just people trying to get along. They didn't want anything special."

"I need to speak with this woman... and the boy. Why won't you help us? At least tell us their names."

"I can't do that, Mrs. Hamrick."

"For heaven's sake why not?"

"Because there's nothing you can do."

Uncle Henry had harnessed the mare to the buggy, thinking that a horse-drawn carriage would look more important and would make a stronger impression. Since the buggy could only carry two people, Amanda went alone with Uncle Henry in search of her brother's wife and son.

Masked by a stand of Chinaberry trees, a row of log cabins came into view. There were more than fifty, neatly whitewashed, with brick chimneys and shingled roofs. They gave the impression of ordered neatness. A main avenue between them and a couple of narrow side streets constituted the village that had once been the slave quarters for one of the biggest and most prestigious plantations in the county. The estate was very extensive with many outbuildings, orchards and fields. As many as three hundred people had lived there during slave times.

The big house and most of the barns, the gin house and mill had been burned during the war and were never rebuilt. It was now occupied by thirty or forty families of freed Negroes, share cropping the almost exhausted fields for an absentee landlord they had never met.

The village had a dark medieval look. Each cabin was enclosed by a palisade of wooden poles and sticks set up into a tight fence that enclosed private chicken and pig yards. Most of the space between them was cultivated into vegetables and several women working in these gardens looked up as they passed. There were half-clad children playing in the dusty street and several men standing with their hands in their pockets. More heads turned, but no one spoke.

At the end of the main street was a bigger, two story house of four or five rooms, which had been leased to the railroad and was being used to board a gang of track workers who were replacing ties along a neglected spur of the M & T. Amanda would later learn that it had been the overseer's house and that the people would rather have seen it stay empty.

Uncle Henry pulled the buggy to a stop beside an old man sitting in a wooden rocking chair, got down and went over to the man. Amanda waited in the carriage. The two men talked and gestured boldly for a few seconds and some others gathered around before Uncle Henry turned back toward the carriage and signaled for Amanda to approach.

"Dis here be ol' Gran-pappy Calvin, an dis here be Sis Elle an' Sis Dora an' Brer Albert and Auntie Mae. Dey noes de story."

Everybody bowed or curtseyed and offered to shake hands. They looked serious, almost sad, Amanda thought, but they seemed eager to talk.

"Mistus Amanda be Mista O'mstid's sista."

Amanda smiled and joined the little procession into the cabin. The interior space was divided into two rooms. There was one window opening, nothing more than a square hole with a sliding wooden shutter. There were two doors, one in front and one in the rear. There was a brick fireplace with a hearth and a few utensils neatly arranged and dwarfed by a heavy iron skillet. There was a table and several simple wooden chairs with cowhide bottoms.

Amanda noticed a mirror over the fireplace and some pictures cut from a magazine tacked on the walls. There was a Bible on the table.

The other room was for sleeping and had pallets on the floor with mattresses stuffed with straw and dried Spanish moss. Clothes were hung from wooden pegs in the walls.

Gran-pappy Calvin carried the rocking chair in from the yard and offered it to Amanda. "No, please that's your chair, please sit in it," Amanda protested and the old man flashed a broad gaping toothless smile and sat down. One of the women brought over a chair for Amanda and she sat facing the old man. "I'm looking for my brother's wife and son," she began, but got no response.

"He cain't hear nuffin' lessun yo' holla real loud" Auntie Mae responded, "an' 'sides he doan 'no nuffin' 'bout no wife an' no son."

"But surely someone knows something," she reacted showing a bit of frustration and turned to Uncle Henry. "Help me, Henry. I only want to do what's right."

Uncle Henry shook his head and looked down at the dirt floor. "We done promis Mattie-Lou dat we doan tole nobody nuffin'."

"Mattie-Lou!" Amanda reacted, "It's Lula! I knew it!"

"You ol' fool!" Auntie Mae was furious. Uncle Henry hung his head and Amanda responded as best she could.

"No, don't be angry I only want to do what's right. Things will work out. You'll see".

"Lady you got no idea what you doin'."

Amanda could sense the atmosphere of fear and mistrust, but couldn't truly appreciate it. She now knew that Lula was Samuel's widow and could only think about returning to Grassy Water. She hardly heard Auntie Mae say, "Nobody be killin' nobody in de ol' days, like tis now. Lord Missie all the darkies here 'bouts got pistols now. Deez be rough times, not like befo'."

At that moment a great commotion outside the cabin drew them all out into the street where a tall handsome Black man sitting high on a magnificent stallion was addressing a growing crowd. He was wearing a dear skin overcoat and gloves with long brown leather English riding boots rolled down at the knee. His squat coffee-brown John Bull top hat matched his complexion and commanded attention. His accent was not from around there.

"Any men here who want to buy or lease land can do it now up in Bolivar County. There's a lot of land being sold off along the east bank of the Mississippi a little north of where the Arkansas River comes in. It's good land, rich virgin land. It needs clearing and cultivating. Come to the depot in Granada tomorrow at noon if you want to learn more."

At first there was no response as each looked at the other and wondered if this smooth talking fancy Black man from some place else could be trusted.

"This is a big opportunity for any man who wants to own land and be his own boss."

Still there was little reaction and the stranger pointed to one man standing in front. "What do you do brother?"

"I's make a garden an I's fish a little bit in de crick."

"And how about you? You still waiting for the Yankees to give you forty acres and a mule?"

I quit dreamin' 'bout dat mule ta wuk on de railroad, but dere be but two, tree days a week..."

"Stop waiting for the White man to give you something for nothing. Cotton's moving upland into the delta. There's opportunity there for any freedman who wants to work." The man sensed a little buzz spread across the crowd and added, "Lease some land, save your money and in two or three years you can own your own farm... be at the depot in Grenada tomorrow at noon."

Chapter Thirteen

It was dark when Amanda returned and Thomas was waiting nervously on the veranda. He had spent the hours of her absence rummaging through the papers and ledgers in Samuel's study, trying to learn all he could about the plantation, what its history was and what it might be worth.

The yield had dropped from over a bale of cotton to the acre before the war to hardly more than a half-bale in the most recent years. The soil was dying; there was no money to fertilize and no way to avoid the conclusion that the future of Grassy Water as a profitable cotton plantation was very dire.

He saw too the problem of having to put together a new labor force for each coming year and how the strain of it had soured every Christmas season for Samuel and had worn down his spirit. Adapting to free labor was maddening since staffing the plantation was far more complex than merely hiring workers.

Few married freedmen would sign on to a year's contract unless provisions were also made for their families and this meant returning to a system that was not much different from slavery. And the very essence of freedom was still new to many unmarried Black men who were very reluctant to surrender their ability to just go if they wanted to, to strike out on their own and not be reminded of the work gangs and the overseers of the hated past.

So Samuel tried share cropping most of his land, but every year his accounts fell further and further out of balance. By the end of reconstruction, Grassy Water was technically bankrupt and only kept afloat by the yearly sale of marginal upland woods to anyone who was willing to clear it; and he sometimes even supplied the axe.

Thomas leaned back in the rocker and closed his eyes. He listened to the sounds of the forest stretching northward and smelled the damp breeze blowing off the cypress swamps and bayous. He slowly slipped away to sleep trying to find some reason why this was all worth it and to understand why his wife was so determined to fight for it.

An hour had passed before Amanda's voice shattered his silent world. "Where is she?"

"Who?" he reacted, jumping to his feet and peering into the dimly moonlit night.

"Lula... she's the one, Tom. She's Samuel's wife."

"She's gone," he answered, struggling to clear his mind, "a while ago. Some man came to get her and she went off with him... in a hurry too I might add."

"Did she say anything?"

"Not to me. Did you see them, Anna?" Thomas asked as his granddaughter appeared in the doorway.

"Yes, like Bumpa said a man ran up to the house from back there," she said, pointing up the road that Amanda had just been on.

"Then what?" Amanda asked intently.

"They just went down the trail along the river." Anna sensed the urgency in her grandmother's voice and asked, "Why, Mimi? What's wrong?"

"Well they couldn't have gotten far," Amanda said looking back to see if Uncle Henry was still there with the buggy.

"We're not going to chase after them at this hour. Whatever it was it can wait until morning," Thomas said assertively. "You've got to slow down, Mandy; I know you're tired."

Amanda stayed silent for a few seconds not sure of what to do next and Thomas added, "I think you should tell us what this is all about."

Thomas and Amanda talked late into the night and agreed that he would go back to Grenada the next day with Uncle Henry to meet with Fly and the man who was making a claim on the estate. She would stay at the house, determined to wait for and confront Lula or as Uncle Henry called her, Mistus Mattie-Lou.

They reached the hand cranked ferry raft that was still the only way to cross the river east of Grenada. It was little more than a floating platform of timbers guided by a strong steel cable strung between two heavily buttressed posts sunk deep into the river bottom on both banks and further braced to landing docks. Another steel cable, wrapped around a drum on the raft itself, connected winches on the two posts, so by turning one of the winches, a person could send the ferry back and forth across the river or propel the raft and cargo across by using the crank on the raft itself. The long ratcheting handle provided just enough mechanical advantage to allow a strong man alone to move a heavy load.

Uncle Henry led the horse onto the raft and Thomas stepped down from the buggy to assist if he could. “Can I help crank her, Uncle?” he asked.

The little Black man hardly heard him and shook his head, but said nothing. He was still deeply troubled by his earlier blunder and his mind was far away.

Thomas went on trying to engage him as best he could. “This is a sturdy ferry. I’ll bet it’s seen a lot of work over the years.”

This time his efforts made some progress as Uncle Henry loved to reminisce about the old days. It was a topic where age had the advantage. He tried to not talk too much, but his friendly and gregarious nature made it impossible. “We doan hab no down river road on dis side. De big road be on Gareau’s side so we needs de ferry fer dat.”

“Did you carry cotton over this ferry?”

“Nossur, rafted it down de river. Mossa de time ta Vicksburg. Befo’ de wah we made plenty a cotton. Steamboats sometime be up here haulin’ it afta de wah, but I ain’t seed dat no mo’. Ceppin’ dis year, jus bout de time de lass fros fell when de water be high I seed a steamboat in de river. I seed it cumin’ on ta da cable dere so I foot it jes ez fas’ as I do an I kep’ hollerin’ but dey don’t pay me no mine. I nebber seed a boat like dat befo’. I wus plum flabbergasted. I seed it prorogin’ roun ‘n roun, cumin’ an’ goin’. Weren’t no sense to it. Frum dat day til now I ax myself what in tarnation wuz dey up to.”

“You have no idea what they were doing?”

Uncle Henry shook his head and added, “It hab a funny name too. I look at it fo’ fi’ time to be shu I got it right, an’ I scratch it out on de rail dere.” Thomas followed the old man’s finger down and read the word, “essayons.”

“That was it, essayons?” The word meant nothing to Thomas who had little interest in the boat, but thought continuing to talk might lead to something useful from the old man who knew much more than he was saying and so he probed a bit more.

“How old are you, Uncle?”

“I cain’t recollect rightly, but I does know I’se old!”

“You must have seen a lot of things change over the years?”

“Yessur, I trable all ‘roun’ wid de wagon an’ I seed lot a changes.”

“What do you make of all this, Uncle Henry? I mean about the plantation. What can you tell me about this partner that Samuel had, this Jean Gareau? Where can we find him?”

“He be gone. Dey skeered de breeches off en em. But he neber be no pardner o’ Marsa Sam... I mean mah imploya... couldn’t ‘pend on em no how. Nossur. Gareau be good fer nuffin’ ceppin’ drinkin’ and gamblin’. He owe ebrybody money ‘till dis here Dinkin sumptin’ buy up all a dat debt and tuk his lan’ fer it.”

“What do you know about Dinkin Sanford?”

“He ain’t no good. I knows dat!”

They had hardly slept. The night was very dark and the noises were strange. When they met in the morning the house was empty and they did their best with breakfast. Now, with her grandmother buried in the minutiae of her brother’s business papers and records, Anna decided to venture out on her own. She watched from the veranda as Uncle Henry’s buggy disappeared with her grandfather down the narrow roadway toward the river and after a time followed lazily until she reached the landing. The empty ferry raft was on the opposite shore. She walked out onto the old wooden dock that had never seen the sun. It was damp and slippery beneath her feet.

She looked down the dark dreamy river, lined with massive trunks and overhung with lush drooping limbs, heavy with wild grapes and Spanish moss. It was an eerie place and yet in some ways it was wonderful. The river was slow there and secluded, but strangely alive. She had never seen, much less heard, so many insects. The night had been filled with the sound of caddis flies hatching all along the river and the splashing of fish striking the surface in search of an easy meal. As the sun rose, humming swarms of midges could be seen dancing low barely above the water enticing an occasional belated rise from a hungry bass.

Anna knew how much her father loved to fly-fish and wished that he could see this place. What fun he would have here she thought as she visualized him eagerly selecting just the right fly to match the hatch and then casting intently toward the shaded shoreline. As her eye wandered along the bank in search of the next rising fish she saw a Black man on the opposite side pulling in lines that had apparently been set out with bait the night before. Hand over hand he hauled in several fat catfish that he collected in a bag, quickly baited his hooks again with what looked like chicken entrails and set them adrift. In a few seconds he was gone.

Before she could think much about the significance of what she had just witnessed, her attention was seized by the squeaking sound of the ferry winch and she looked up to see it creeping fitfully toward her. Anna couldn't make out the face of the woman bent over the crank, but she instantly recognized the white wedding dress in the basket beside her.

The girl looked up when she felt the load on the winch lighten and saw Anna waving with one arm while cranking the drum at her end with the other. Angeline suddenly froze, holding tight to the handle. The raft rattled to a stop, rocking back and forth as though trying to rotate on some kind of pivot, to turn and go back, the cable clapping its objection against the sides of winch post.

"Angeline, it's Anna." She yelled as loudly as she could, but the girl stood stiffly in place pretending not to hear.

"It's Anna, from last night. What's wrong?"

A few more seconds passed in silence. Angeline Havens had no where to run and besides there was no point in it anyway so she waved back as though nothing were wrong and started turning the drum again. She didn't have the fear of Whites and sense of secrecy and caution that clouded everything the older generations did. She was born free and had no deep scars from slavery. Her mother was an educated White woman who had come south to Mississippi with the Quakers to teach school, long before the war had ended. Shunned and ridiculed by southern society, her mother boarded for several years with a Black clergyman and his family in Vicksburg, where she met and later married the minister's son.

Angeline never knew her father. Her mother never talked about him and she never felt the need to know about him. Her earliest memories are of this place where her mother came to teach in a small school house that Samuel and some others had built in Grenada. She had a happy childhood. Her mother's salary, supplemented by the Freedmen's Bureau, was adequate to provide a comfortable life and she went to regular school. She loved to read and her childhood was filled with fantasy and the wonders of imagination.

"I was hoping to see you again. Why did you run off last night?"

"Oh... It was a bad time. I didn't want to be in the way."

"I wanted you to meet my grandparents. You should have stayed. Come back to the house with me. My grandfather has gone, but my grandmother is there. I know she'd love to meet you." When the girl didn't answer Anna added, "You've probably come to see Lula. I'm sorry I didn't mean to intrude. Of course... you've come to see Lula. I'm sorry," she said again.

"No, don't be sorry," Angeline answered. "I'm going to Aunt Effie's to bring her the dress. Lula's not at Grassy Water..." She paused as she rethought her response. "Anyway, I saw her this morning already."

Anna's eyes lit as she looked down at the wedding dress overflowing the basket in the girl's hand. "Did Lula like it?" she asked in a way that showed such sincerity that Angeline lost what little sense of caution she had left. They were now just two girls talking about getting married.

"Walk with me a ways," Angeline said with a wide-eyed smile.

"Tell me about him," Anna almost squealed.

"About whom?" she teased.

"About him... you know who."

"His name is... Caleb... Pritchard."

"And?"

"And...what?"

"And is he the sweetest and the handsomest?"

"No... but he is the smartest and the best."

"And..."

"And... I don't know what you want me to say."

"Are you in love with him?"

"Of course I love him. Can't you tell?"

"You're... really... in love with him!"

"I am... And he loves me, Anna. I know it just by the way he looks at me." The two girls walked on for a few steps each dancing in her own dreams, before Angeline asked, "Have you ever been in love?"

"No... but I know I will be someday. It must be so wonderful to find the one you love and not just because your father thinks it's the best match or because you'd better hurry up before you're an old maid. How old is he?" she added to push away the unhappy thought.

"He's twenty-two."

"What does he do? Where will you live?"

"He's so ambitious, Anna. He hasn't got much, but just listening to him talk, his dreams are so romantic that I know I'd go with him anywhere."

"And you're just... eighteen?"

"Nineteen."

"Why, it's perfect. The men back home are always so much older. They always think they have to be established first so they can make a good proposition to the family. Thank God my father's not like that. It seems so exciting to start out with nothing and work together for the future."

"He wants to start a farm somewhere away from here, further up in the delta. He knows all about cotton. He's lived with it all of his life. Some of his friends have already gone up there and they're cutting timber. You can lease land from the railroad, clear it for yourself and have a place of your own where nobody will bother you. He says that new railroads are bound to crisscross all over the place in few years and by then we'll be ready to ship cotton."

"What do your parents think of that?"

"Both of our fathers are dead. We're going to bring my mother with us. Lula won't go; she'll probably stay with Aunt Effie."

Anna stopped dead in her tracks. "Lula is Caleb's mother?"

"I don't know why she keeps hiding it," Angeline answered having earlier decided not to try to avoid the inevitable any longer. What did it matter anyway? "Her name is Mattie-Lou Pritchard."

"And she was Samuel's wife, wasn't she?"

Angeline's silence confirmed Anna's conclusion. Her mind was running rapidly having seemingly found the son and solved the riddle that so much concerned her grandmother. Her thoughts flowed freely into words. "My Great Uncle Samuel was Caleb's father and he was named after Samuel's brother, the one that died. God... Angeline... that means that Caleb and I are cousins or something. His father was my grandmother's brother. What does that make us?"

"Cousins I think, once removed I think they call it."

"And then after you marry my cousin we'll be cousins too... or step cousins or cousins by marriage," she said laughing and naively throwing her arms around Angeline who was suddenly visibly less exuberant.

"But my grandmother came down here to find a way to get the plantation for Caleb," Anna went on excitedly. "Does he know that? Won't that be great?"

Angeline returned to reality. "He doesn't want it. It's not worth it. They won't let him have it anyway. It was his father's plan and Caleb went along with it, but he never believed it."

"But, why not?"

"There's something here that somebody wants and they're going to get it."

"But it rightfully belongs to him."

"Says who?"

"The law I would hope."

"We're Black, Anna."

There was a hard edge to the remark and the mood darkened; the flush of youthful friendship was dampened. They walked on side by side into the dense wood for a long time in silence. The forest road was little more than an old Choctaw game trail widened into a bridal path winding a serpentine course out of the swamps and bayous of the Yalobusha bottom into the untapped upland. It stretched north for miles through the seemingly endless stands of oaks and beeches before swinging east to join the Natchez Trace, then on across Alabama and Tennessee.

There was something frightening in its vast seclusion and silence while at the same time exhilarating and uplifting. The virgin forest was old, with stately trees set apart so as not to impede a person walking through them, but taken together they made an opaque wall, impossible to see through that hemmed in the road and imprisoned its travelers.

For Angeline the forest was a metaphor. "Midway upon the journey of our life," she closed her eyes and began, "I found myself within a forest dark... For the straightforward pathway had been lost..."

"Ah me! How hard a thing it is to say," Anna continued as it awakened her memory. "It's Dante; you know Dante?"

Angeline smiled and asked, "Are you surprised?" Anna had no response and the girl went on. "What was this forest savage, rough, and stern...? Which in the very thought renews the fear... So bitter is it, death is little more..."

"But you should finish it, Angeline. Remember the last lines... But of the... good... to treat which there I found..."

CHAPTER FOURTEEN

Fly's office was unusually spacious and bright. The heavy drapes were thrown back on the two expansive east facing plate glass windows and the morning sun streamed across the carpeted floor. For a law office, the room was strangely without books and was dominated by one massive red oak desk that covered most of the wall beside the fireplace. The workspace was uncluttered and the dozens of pigeon holes and compartments in the huge hutch top that rose half-way to the ceiling were neatly organized. It was an imposing desk meant to make a statement about the status and demeanor of the man who owned it. But, for all of that, it was the typewriter on the small unassuming credenza at the back of the room that first caught Thomas's eye.

"I see you've adopted the latest in typewriting equipment, Mr. Fly."

"Indeed, Mr. Hamrick," the lawyer responded swinging around in his swivel chair and politely standing. "That, I am proud to say, is a Remington number-two typewriter, the finest and most modern made. We may be in the sticks... but we not hicks," he quipped with a wink and a smile, accustomed to disarming strangers with homey warmth.

"I didn't intend to imply that you were, sir," Thomas replied, nodding politely to the other man in the room and then added, "In fact that is the first new Remington I have actually seen, other than in pictures and advertisements. I know my son has begun to use one in the business, but in my day we had nothing like that; everything was done by hand."

"Well, with a good operator the machine is far superior, Mr. Hamrick and with the new greaseless carbon paper, we get as many as six or seven perfect copies. We do a lot of letters in a law office as you might imagine and making copies was always a nuisance."

The usual introductory small talk continued for a few more seconds before Fly got down to business. "Let me introduce you to Mr. Clayton Barr," he began, motioning for the other man to step forward. "Mr. Barr represents Mr. Dinkin Sanford and has come here prepared to make you and Mrs. Hamrick an offer to settle the contract obligations that are delaying her inheritance."

The two men shook hands. Barr was a tall slender man. To Thomas he seemed weak, almost dainty, his hands were soft and his grip was delicate. It was the kind of limp, languid handshake that for Thomas was instantly repugnant.

"Would you like a cigar, Mr. Hamrick, or perhaps a glass of Sherry?" Fly asked.

"Let's get right to it, Mr. Fly," Thomas answered, already unwilling to accept anything on face value. "Perhaps you could explain this... contract obligation... that is holding up the inheritance as you put it."

Barr handed Thomas the papers, signed and properly sealed, on which it was written exactly as Fly had said. "Everything is quite in order, Mr. Hamrick."

The three men sat and when, after a minute or two, Thomas looked up from the documents, Clayton Barr spoke. "As you can see Mr. Hamrick, the value of the property was set at four thousand dollars by the commission appointed pursuant to the Mississippi Debt and Valuation Law as stipulated in the contract. My client wishes to exercise his option and is now prepared to meet the terms of that agreement, which as you can see grant him the right to buy the estate for this value." Barr paused briefly before announcing with a rising tone of enthusiasm, "Hence I am authorized to pay you the sum of four thousand dollars."

Thomas knew that Amanda felt duty-bound to honor her brother's dying wish. He didn't like Barr and was already beginning to become suspicious of Fly. He didn't believe anything they told him and was unsure about what to do next. His best strategy was to stall. "Well, as you gentlemen know, this will be my wife's decision..."

"She really has no choice, Mr. Hamrick," Fly quickly responded. "In the end it will be ordered by the court. The law is clear. This contract is enforceable. I suggest you settle it now and save yourself and your lovely wife the time and trouble of adjudicating it."

"I understand your position, Mr. Fly and I appreciate your advice, but you must understand that this is not my wife's wish and she isn't satisfied that she fully understands where the truth lies in these matters. She'll need some time to sort out all the details. For example, we'd like to talk to this man, Gareau. Where can we find him?"

Before Fly could answer, Clayton Barr spoke. "Mr. Sanford has authorized me to add five hundred dollars to the sum in consideration for settling this privately and expeditiously..."

"That's very generous, Mr. Barr, but as I said before, it's my wife's decision," Thomas interrupted and then repeated his question. "Where is Jean Gareau?"

"I don't know," Fly answered impatiently before Barr could respond. "Gone west I think, Oklahoma maybe."

Thomas didn't like the glib answer and was now convinced that he could not trust Graham Fly. "Is Grenada the county seat?" he asked in a tone that said he had heard enough and was about to end the meeting.

"Yes."

"Then I should find the Register of Deeds here?"

The two lawyers exchanged glances and Fly restructured his advice to settle the matter out of court. "Mr. Hamrick, as executor of the will I am ethically bound to act in the best interests of the heirs. I take this responsibility very seriously and if I believed that there was any chance of prevailing I would not hesitate to recommend that Mrs. Hamrick litigate this case. But there is no chance."

Barr then asked, "Is it more money you want, Mr. Hamrick? If it is I am prepared to commit Mr. Sanford to an increase in the offer to five thousand dollars."

Fly buttressed Barr's new proposal with more homey emotion. "Talk some sense to her man, you can't win this. Take the money and go home."

But, Thomas had already drawn his conclusions and asked again tersely. "Where can I find the Register of Deeds?"

The three men stood simultaneously, but no one extended his hand. A few awkward seconds passed before Fly answered. "Go to the old court house, to the office of the Clerk of Chancery. He is the Register of Deeds and maintains all the public records." Then, as Thomas turned to leave, Fly added, "You're a Yankee, Hamrick. It wouldn't do to do too much snooping around."

"Is that a threat, Mr. Fly?"

"No, my friend. It's just good advice that's all. There are those here about that don't take kindly to outsiders making trouble."

"Good day, sir."

Thomas was sure that these men were tied together and that for some reason they were conspiring to con him; he didn't like it. He was angry, but had no recourse. His options were few and he knew it as he left the lawyer's office and crossed the street to the buggy where Uncle Henry was waiting.

Thomas Hamrick was in a strange place, far from home. He was perplexed and without a plan, but he knew that he couldn't let that stop him. What he needed were allies and he could think of only one. There was in fact, at that moment, only one person in Mississippi he could turn to, the only one instinct told him to trust, Uncle Henry.

The old man listened to Thomas as he recounted every detail of the story, but said nothing. As he spoke, he watched the former slave, who couldn't read a single word, fiddling with a newspaper. The symbolic futility of it entered his mind and he felt discouraged. He didn't know when to stop or how to judge whether Uncle Henry even understood him. After all, what could this man possibly know about the law? This is hopeless, he thought to himself. How could he have anything worthwhile to say? I'm just wasting my time? Maybe we should just take the money and go home.

When Thomas finally stopped, convinced that he had exhausted every way of simplifying it and saying it, he looked expectantly at the Black buggy driver, but with little hope for more than a trite anecdote delivered in almost unintelligible dialect. He surely didn't expect the voice of Socrates, but that was closer to what he got.

Uncle Henry handed Thomas a dollar bill, a brand new silver certificate that had been kept carefully folded in his vest pocket. "See dat dere?" he asked pointing to a signature on the face of the bill. Thomas read the name, "B.K. Bruce," and Henry said, "ebrybody roun' here know who dat be?"

"It says that he is Register of the Treasury of the United States," Thomas said, humoring the old man, while wondering where it would lead and what it could possibly have to do with his problem.

"I wants yo' ter know... dat dere be a Negro man," he said with an obvious hint of pride. "Dis money be good fer nuffin'... lessun Mr. Blanche Kelso Bruce sign on it."

Thomas could see the emotional impact that such a successful and accomplished Black had on Uncle Henry and had no intention of diminishing its significance, but began to conclude that expecting any real help from him was only wishful thinking.

Then Uncle Henry handed Thomas a copy of the newspaper he was holding. It was Saturday and the Grenada Sentinel had just been released. "You wants ta read dis here. Den yo' know what ta do."

> *Former United States Senator Blanche Kelso Bruce will stop in Grenada this afternoon on his way to Jackson. He is expected to speak briefly at the depot. The purpose of his visit is not fully understood, but it is causing quite a stir among the Black population. Sheriff Smith has assured the people of Grenada that he is fully prepared to maintain order should that become necessary...*

Thomas understood immediately and smiled. It was more than a flicker of hope, it was a real possibility. Bruce was an influential man with connections and the fact that he was Black offered considerable comfort that in this matter he could be trusted. Thomas decided to wait to see if he could talk with Blanche Kelso

Bruce. He needed allies; perhaps now, thanks to Uncle Henry, he might find one.

The hours slipped away while Amanda searched the documents and papers that filled Samuel's study and business room. The whole financial history of Grassy Water was laid before her. At first it was all a confused maze of receipts and invoices, but the anecdotal notes and comments scribbled in the margins and open spaces gradually began to tell the story of the cotton contagion that consumed the South in the decades before the war.

"Everywhere you look there's cotton," she read over and over again. The roads were glutted with wagons stacked with bulging bales; boats and barges disappeared under it. The river towns were buried in it; every open lot was piled high with it and laments about the price of it were on everybody's lips.

"The only other thing you see on the roads are planters moving west with their slaves looking for new land to grow it on." She repeated his words softly to herself and felt their unmistakable implication for Samuel's story and its inevitable ending.

Then she learned that the market collapsed. Prices fell to only a few cents a pound and her brother saw plantations all around him fall into bankruptcy. From that point it was a basic struggle for the very survival of the once mighty cotton kingdom. After that, Grassy Water had only a few profitable years, during the occupation and early reconstruction, but for the most part breaking even, or almost even, was the most he could hope for.

Amanda was captivated by her brother's determination to find a way to return his plantation to the golden age. She could see his growing obsession to sink his roots somewhere and to leave a proud legacy to his son. She learned that in the most recent years, the quest to bring the plantation back to profitability was all consuming for him as he experimented with hoes versus plows and horses versus mules, tried every kind of improved strain of cotton, deeper rooted, drought tolerant, disease resistant; nothing worked, nothing that is except fertilizer. It was the fertility of the land of course that was ebbing way. Cotton seed waste was all he had and he used it along with every bit of barnyard manure he could get. But it was never enough. He knew about guano, but it was too expensive.

Then, in the back of the bottom drawer she found an envelope and Samuel's original Will and Testament written two decades earlier. She read it slowly.

The last Will and Testament of Samuel Olmstead, of the County of Grenada in the State of Mississippi

I, Samuel Olmstead, considering the danger of these uncertain times and the weakness of this frail body, and being of sound mind, do declare this to be my last will and testament.

I give and bequeath unto my wife, Mattie-Lou (Prichard) Olmstead, all of my real estate and possessions of whatever kind or nature, to have and hold the same during her natural life and to be administered at her sole discretion.

Upon her death the remainder shall go to and belong to my son, Caleb Olmstead. Should his death precede hers I bequeath whatever remains of my estate to be divided among her heirs in whatever manner she should declare to be her wish.

Knowing that my marriage to a woman of color will cause my last wishes to be ignored and even scorned compels me to add the following statement to my will. As my love for and marriage to Mattie-Lou Prichard was and is a personal and private matter I hold any law invalidating it to deny her rightful inheritance to be null and void.

Although I do not owe anyone an explanation for my actions I feel driven by duty to my wife and son to make this simple one. I married the woman I love. How can this be wrong? I cannot ignore my conscience and I will not jeopardize my salvation by yielding to philandering hypocrites. Let Matthew remind you of the judgment you face:

...Thus have ye made the commandment of God of none effect by your tradition. ...Ye hypocrites, well did Isaias prophesy of you, saying, ...This people draweth nigh unto me with their mouth, and honoureth me with their lips; but their heart is far from me. ...But in vain they do worship me, teaching for doctrines the commandments of men.

In witness whereof I have hereunto set my hand this 12th day of May, A. D. 1863.

Samuel Olmstead

This instrument was declared by the testator, Mr. Samuel Olmstead to be his last will and testament, and we sign our names hereto as attesting witnesses.

Jean Gareau, Grenada Mississippi
Hon. Joseph Johnston, Esq.. Grenada, Mississippi

Amanda returned the single sheet of paper to its resting place sat quietly for a few seconds and then rummaged on. She next uncovered the doctor's bills, prescriptions and hospital records and the realization struck her that she didn't yet know how her brother had died. She scrambled anxiously, at the same time both attracted and repelled, through the stacks of paper, gradually pulling the picture into focus.

It began with complaints of dyspepsia and vomiting treated with the usual tonics and palliatives until it led to the dreaded diagnosis of stomach cancer. The radical surgery intended to restore his health removed several large tumors, but serious damage to the gastric wall left him weak and barely able to eat. He was told that he had no more than a few weeks to live. Massive amounts of morphine were prescribed to keep him comfortable, but the stupor they caused so interfered with his ability to settle his affairs that he refused to take it. Amanda clearly felt her brother's pain and understood the frantic urgency of his efforts to find her and to tell her his story, magnifying a thousand times the weight of responsibility she carried. She knew he suffered terribly and that in the end he welcomed death.

Suddenly her granddaughter's voice commanded her consciousness and pulled her back. "Mimi, there you are. You'll never guess..."

"Anna!" Amanda responded without waiting as she realized that her granddaughter had been gone all morning. "Where have you been? I was worried." Her words were an expression of her own feelings of fear and alienation at that moment as she pulled her granddaughter tightly into her arms.

"I was with Angeline..."

"You've got to be careful, Anna. We don't know these people."

"She's really nice, Mimi. We hit it off really well and I found out something that you're going to be interested in." Amanda said nothing and Anna continued, "Angeline is going to marry Uncle Samuel's son."

"What?"

"Next Saturday if you can believe it."

"Did you talk to him?" Amanda reacted with immediate excitement.

"Not yet, but I know his name is Caleb and Angeline is taking me to meet him this afternoon. And guess what else," Anna added with a sly smile. This time not waiting for a response she went on, "Lula is his mother!"

"Why are they hiding from us, Anna? I don't understand it."

The search for some independent verification of the assertion that there had been a partnership agreement giving Jean Gareau a claim to Grassy Water led Thomas to the Register of Deeds in Grenada. There was no indication of any such contract anywhere in the memoir and it ran contrary to Samuel's fervent and oft repeated wish to see his estate passed on to his son. It just didn't seem likely that he would have done it.

It was only a few steps from Fly's office to the courthouse and Thomas decided to walk. Uncle Henry stayed with the buggy. There were hundreds of Blacks coming into town that day in anticipation of the arrival of Blanche Kelso Bruce and rumors that he was planning to announce that the federal government would finally make good on the mystical promise of forty acres and a mule for every freedman. Before he left, Thomas asked Uncle Henry why this myth persisted when it was obvious after all these years that there would never be forty acres and a mule.

"Mos cullud folks haint got nuffin' in de worl'. Dey always be wantin' em te git. But dey haint got no place te git to."

The assistant to the Clerk of Chancery was friendly and helpful. "You'll have to excuse us, Mr. Hamrick; as you can see we are in the midst of copying and cataloging our records. Our new courthouse will be open in less than a year and we want to be ready for the move."

Thomas glanced at the stacks of dusty books and boxes, but his mind was fully preoccupied and he went directly to his request to see the land records pertaining to Samuel's estate.

"The deed has been duly registered along with certification that a patent had been issued by the Land Office in Washington," the clerk reported, turning the big book with faded hand written entries toward Thomas so he could see for himself. "The official sealed certificate should be among the decedent's effects."

"Well, we haven't found it, but..."

"It doesn't matter. It's all very proper, Mr. Hamrick. Mr. Samuel Olmstead was the holder of the first title to this tract. He had a land patent from the government of the United States."

"I don't see anything here about any limitations on the title to this property, no liens or mortgages. I'm trying to verify the existence of a claim on this land that apparently occurred many years ago. Wouldn't that be important enough to record?"

"Could be... but, people don't like to pay the clerk's fees, Mr. Hamrick," the man answered with a smile. "That's all. It's not unusual not to record various forms of contracts, such as leases, partnerships so I wouldn't read much into that."

"So... such a contract could still exist and this may not be a free title even though it's recorded as such?"

"Absolutely," the man responded and added inquisitively, "There seems to be quite an interest in this particular estate."

"How do you mean, sir?"

"There were two men here yesterday inquiring about it as well. They even asked to see the official map of the survey. They asked a lot of questions about the swamps and different rivers and creeks up there along the Yalobusha bottom. They even asked if we had topographical survey maps."

"Who were these men?"

"I don't remember their names, but they said they were Pinkerton Detectives."

"Do you know where they went or what they were after?"

"No. I told them we don't have topographical maps here and suggested they go to Jackson or maybe try the army engineers down in Vicksburg, but that's about it."

"Tell me sir," Thomas went on as an after thought. "What's all the commotion here about?"

"Apparently we're going to have a speech down at the depot later today. Old Senator Bruce, he's a Negro you know, is going to address his people about getting land here in Mississippi. There's been a push lately by some to get a lot of these Blacks that are just hanging around with no job to go after government land in the West. I guess he's got other ideas."

Thomas probed for anything he could learn that might help him fashion an appeal to the former Senator. "What sort of ideas?"

"Well there's empty land all across the delta and railroad right-of-way land that can be leased or bought. I hear he's also breaking up some of his own property and selling it off into small farms." Thomas just nodded and the clerk added, "He's making a lot of people nervous; I can tell you that."

Chapter Fifteen

The sound of voices could be heard wafting in on the breeze from far away in the forest as the two girls walked along the river's edge. "I don't think that could be them," Angeline remarked, "it's too close."

"I'm so glad I brought my Balmorals," Anna remarked looking down at her new boots.

"We always thought you proper White city girls only wore thin slippers or heels," Angeline teased.

"It's almost laughable isn't it, but my mother would have traipsed through these woods in slippers," Anna answered. "But then she had to be bewitching and helpless."

"Lovely and fragile," Angeline quipped mockingly and they both laughed feeling more and more at ease together. "The soles must be a half-inch thick and with the military heels all you need is a red petticoat," she went on.

"I've got one on!" Anna said giggling and hiking her dress to show. "Everybody wears them with big old boots back home. It's the style now. They call it muscular feminism."

"What!"

"Oh, yes... and they put holes in them and scuffs all over them to look like they've been trudging over the Himalayas or something, when they've never stepped off of a Fifth Avenue sidewalk." Angeline just smiled and Anna went on. "Girl's in New York would die for that homespun gown you're wearing."

"You're kidding!"

"I'm serious. It's all the rage."

There was no wagon road on that side of the Yalobusha, but the heavily trodden trail was sure-footed and secure. It led to a place where the river widened just before a small creek flowed in from the north and where the water was shallow and slow moving. The creek had, over the centuries, created a small sand bar and the fast current of the early spring had eroded several gullies and holes in the bottom. It was a perfect spot to seine for shad.

"There's going to be a fish-fry too, I guess," Angeline remarked as they came upon a group of half-clad men and boys busily rushing about in some sort of loosely coordinated combination of fun and chaos that fascinated Anna; they stopped to watch.

There was a net stretched across the river attached to two poles held by two men who were slowly walking up stream toward a line of boys stretching in a blockade across the river ahead of them, some of the little ones nearly up to their necks in the water. Cork floats held up one edge of the net while the other edge dragged along the bottom, held down by stones sewn into the netting. It was a moving fence of sorts, sweeping everything ahead of it.

As the two men approached the blockade line, the boys began to holler and jump around slapping and splashing the water with sticks to turn the fleeing fish back into the waiting trap. Then one of the men stopped and held his pole firm to form a pivot while the other slowly swung around wading across the stream, making a circle until the two poles met, wrapping everything up within it. Some other men, who had been following in the water behind to free any snags on the bottom that might hang up the net, grabbed hold of it and began to haul it onto the bank. Suddenly the flashing silver of flopping fish in the bright sunlight could be seen and a rousing cheer roared up from everyone. Even Anna and Angeline felt the wave of excitement and clapped enthusiastically. The haul was heavy and after sifting out a few thankful frogs and turtles several baskets were filled for the fish-fry.

"Are they going to bring that to the party?" Anna asked.

"It looks that way. There'll be some pork roasting too I'll bet. Only... we like to call it a frolic. It goes back before the war and was one of the only ways that slaves could cut loose once in a while."

As they turned to go, Anna looked back at the river; the work was done and with water splashing and bodies flying every which way it was time for the fun to begin. "I guess frolic is the right name for it!"

"You'll see, Anna; it'll be lots of fun."

They followed the men carrying the baskets of fish and soon came upon a grove in the wood. It was just a clearing under some trees, but it made a kind of shady forest arbor where countless Saturday night frolics had been held for decades. The ground was flattened and packed hard from so many years of use. Then just before the dancing was to begin it was spread over with something soft and damp to make it easy to slip and slide on.

"It's wheat bran, I think," Angeline commented noticing Anna's interest.

"We got no wheat," a man spreading the stuff laughed. "Dis here be corn sweepin' from de gristmill. Works jus fine."

A couple of wagons and mules that had packed in the kindling and split wood for the fires were around, but most of the people had walked, some a goodly way. Big fire pits had been dug in the open ground and some of the men had since early morning been preparing the pig for the feast. Shovelfuls of glowing coals and embers were dug out of the pits and piled on flat stones under the big black iron pans where some women were waiting for the fish to be cleaned.

Dozens more, young and old, were milling expectantly along the edge of the dance floor waiting patiently for the signal that the dressing was down and the dancing could begin. "Ring up dat fiddle," the man with the broom shouted, "an' shuffle yo' feet." It was the signal they were all waiting for and a roar that must have echoed for miles rose up all around.

Anna was captivated by the energy and exuberance of the celebration. It was pure unencumbered fun just as Angeline had promised and was such as she had never experienced before. There was no pretense or reservation, no worry about appearances or social consequences. It seemed like everybody was dancing or patting out a rhythm.

"S'lute yo' pardners... forward an' back... turn yo' corner... right hand roun'... swing yo' pardners, roun' agin..."

"They always start off with that old-time square dance," Angeline said leaning over to be better heard, "but it doesn't take long once those fiddles and banjoes get going before they just fancy-foot, let their feet fly and high-step off by themselves doing buck dances and pigeon-wings. You'll see."

The two girls stood along the side as more and more people flooded onto the dirt dance floor. "Get shufflin' yo' foots dere," an elderly woman said to the girls. "Why yo' chilluns doan no nuffin' 'bout dancin'." Then the woman took Anna by the hands and pulled her into the throng of swinging arms and legs. "Jus' let yo' foots go chile an' whirl aroun'. Yo' doan need no pardner."

Angeline seemed thoroughly entertained watching Anna try her best and was happy that her new White friend didn't seem at all snooty or uncomfortable. But... after a few minutes she thought Anna needed to be rescued. "Thank you, Granny Tine. We'll come back later, but we've got to go find Caleb, OK?"

The old woman smiled and cradled Anna's face in her soft wrinkled hands. "Let ol' Granny Tine be a lessun to yo' chile. De fust time I'se be at de frolic I'se be jus' like you. I jus' sit aroun' an doan dance none. I haint neber gwine a do dat no mo. Seem like White folkses needs dat lessun more en anybody."

Thomas had been waiting for over an hour when the train arrived and Blanche Kelso Bruce stepped down from his private car. He was a light skinned mulatto man of stocky build and distinguished look and as he climbed onto the luggage platform to address the large crowd that had gathered, Thomas had pause to wonder just what an American Negro person really was. This man displayed only the slightest hint of his African heritage and Thomas had seen many so-called Negroes who had blue eyes and whose skin was lighter than his own. The effects of centuries of racial mixing had so blended the blood of these two races as to often make the whole distinction between White and Black a kind of make-believe.

Thomas listened from the back as Bruce spoke about patience and how hard work would pay off, but the crowd was restless and never really settled down. They groaned at the news that once again the dream of free land had been dashed and were visibly unimpressed by his offer to sell his own land at very reasonable prices to any freedman who wanted to start a small farm. Many turned and left before he had finished.

Thomas saw the look of stoic disappointment in Bruce's eyes as he approached and introduced himself. "Senator Bruce," he began with a polite bow. "My name is Thomas Hamrick. May I have a word with you, sir?"

"How can I help you, Mr. Hamrick?" Bruce replied with a friendly smile, accustomed to being recognized and spoken to by strangers.

"I enjoyed your speech, sir," Thomas began with friendly compliments. "Very generous of you to offer your own land to help some of these men get a start."

"Well, one does what one can," Bruce responded with a hint of sadness. "I only wish I had more influence with them. They come to look at me, gawk even some would say, but they don't listen. I know I'm not really one of them and they don't fully trust me." He paused as though carefully weighing his next remark. "Some of them even say I'm too White. Isn't that strange, Mr. Hamrick?"

Thomas didn't answer, but the man's words so fully blended with his own observation that for a moment he wanted to pursue it. Then he wisely reconsidered, judging that so new an acquaintance would surely find it presumptuous.

For the next few minutes Thomas explained his problem and then asked for the Senator's opinion and counsel. "I would deeply appreciate any guidance you could offer in this matter."

"There is a young lawyer, a graduate of Howard University Law School, named Virgil Chambers, now practicing in Jackson," Bruce said without the slightest hesitation. "Have you heard of Howard University, Mr. Hamrick?"

"No, sir; I don't believe that I have."

"You will," Bruce responded.

Thomas nodded, but said nothing, nudging Bruce back to his original thought, "I think he may be the only African-American attorney in Mississippi," Bruce started again. "He's a brilliant young man, still brimming with idealism. I suggest you talk to him."

"Virgil Chambers... and he's... in Jackson you say?" Thomas repeated and then asked, "Could you write me a note of introduction perhaps?"

"I can do better than that, Mr. Hamrick. If you'd like to accompany me to Jackson, I'll introduce you to him myself."

Angeline shook her head in affectionate disdain, while pulling Anna with her though the crowd. "He'll be at the barbeque pit mopping the pig. He thinks he's a master pig roaster."

On the downwind side of the clearing a pit that looked large enough to roast an ox had been dug in which a wood fire had been kept burning for hours. After the flames had died down and a massive bed of hot charcoal had accumulated, a section of wrought iron fence had been laid across it to form a barbecue grill. By adding an occasional shovelful of fresh charcoal the pit could be kept hot indefinitely.

The pig had been cleaned, dressed and prepared by splitting the rib cage and unfolding it like a big book. The skin on the backbone was left intact and the whole thing spiced and set skin-side down on the grill.

Next to the sizzling slab of meat, near the edge of the fire, was a big pot simmering with a secret mix of liquids and spices known only to Granny Mo. It was the rotating duty of several assistants to continuously mop this sauce over the roasting meat. The tool of choice was a mass of cheese cloth wrapped and tied to the end of a shortened broom handle.

"Prop that end up there," Caleb commanded and two others pried the grate up with a pole and placed some stones under it. The height of the pig over the fire was critical and it was raised or lowered to maintain an even slow cooking that after about eight hours would render the meat juicy and succulent. It was also important to keep the grate tilted up slightly so most of the dripping juices would run off at one end and some could be caught in a pan to be returned to the basting pot.

The girls waited and watched while Caleb lathered the meat with the buttery brown sauce making sure that every crack and crevice was properly flooded. "He's very cute," Anna said raising her brows and Angeline smiled.

They caught his eye, but he was not happy seeing Anna there so he stalled, checking the dripping pan and stirring the sauce pot. Finally, pretending to notice for the first time, he looked up.

"Cal, this is your cousin, Anna."

He exhaled derisively through his nose and quipped, "so I hear; hello... cousin... Anna," he didn't look at her and responded snidely while turning back toward the fire.

"That really smells good," Anna said innocently trying to encourage her way into a conversation. "This is a fabulous... frolic?"

"Just like slave time," he responded in a caustic tone that was obvious even though his back was turned. "All we need are the patrollers to come and bust it up. Or today it would be the KKK wouldn't it?"

Anna raised her eyebrows again and looked at Angeline who said, "Please, Cal, don't do this."

Caleb turned back and said, "What the hell did you bring her here for? What do you think you're going to get from all of this?"

"She's nice, Cal. They're all nice and friendly; they only want to help us."

Caleb wasn't listening and shot his venom right at Anna. "Why don't you go back where you came from... cousin? Go back home, back up North. You can tell all your friends how you ate pig meat and danced with all the coons down in Mississippi; that is what you call us back home isn't it?"

"Stop it, Cal, she's not like that," Angeline interrupted aggressively.

"I think I should go," Anna said, suddenly frightened at being left alone there and not knowing what Angeline would do. She fought back tears and was afraid to speak lest she burst out crying. Her friend noticed.

"You should be ashamed of yourself, Caleb Pritchard," Angeline scolded. "We're going home." She turned back to Anna and said sincerely, "I'm so sorry for this, Anna. He's not mean like that, really."

As the two turned to walk away, Caleb called out, "Wait!"

"Go back and baste your pig," Angeline shot back, "you deserve each other."

"You can't go back alone now it's already getting dark, I'll go with you," Caleb cautioned, but Angeline saw right through his ruse. He was sorry for what he had said, he knew it was wrong and that Anna didn't deserve it, but had great difficulty apologizing.

"My hero," she taunted and turned her back on him. "Don't bother."

"Oh, please," Anna implored. "I don't want to be in the middle of this. I feel awful. It's nothing, please let him come."

"He will anyway," Angeline whispered pushing Anna ahead of her through the crowd.

Caleb followed them for about a mile before Angeline stopped and turned back toward him. "I hope you've thought about it, Caleb."

At first he tried to deflect the issue. "Can't you see it's no use? Do you think they're going to let me be a gentleman farmer at Grassy Water, right here in Grenada? We've got to go upcountry. That's where our future will be. It just isn't going to work here, can't you see that?"

"That's not what I'm talking about, Cal and you know it." she shot back. "I don't give a damn about Grassy Water." She paused to let him respond only vaguely sensing the depth of the conflict he was coping with.

From the earliest arrival of Whites in the new world, the mixing of races was common and everywhere, but it was only in the English speaking places that the fathers disowned their children and denounced the human condition that they were so actively creating. This had become a complicated problem all through the nation, North and South, where the mixed blood population became so large that the love of some White fathers for their biracial children threatened to unleash a social revolution.

Samuel Olmstead vowed that he would never abandon his child, but in the end that is exactly what he did. It was the pain of knowing it that plagued him in his death and drove him to find a way to redeem himself. He never realized what it was doing to his son.

Even though his parents were legally married during the reconstruction and they had lived together in common law bond for many years before that, his mother was always looked upon as a "fancy girl" whose social standing was tied to the status of her White gentleman and her babies no more than tools to cement and safeguard her position. It was an all too common story, but for Samuel and Mattie it wasn't true. They were deeply in love and together at Grassy Water for almost a half-century, isolated and insulated from the outside world.

Caleb, their last and only surviving child was born during the war and with victory for the Union they dreamed of a new world dawning for him. Miraculously at first it all seemed possible, too good to be true in fact. But then the dream was shattered as redemption and Jim Crow cruelly took it all away. The backlash was devastating. Not only was their marriage declared incestuous and void, but they were accused of lascivious and lewd conduct and their son was cited as living proof.

Afraid that Mattie would be arrested, Samuel sent sixteen year-old Caleb to live with his aunt Effie and swore that he was not the boy's father. All of this confused Caleb and caused him to question who he really was and where he really belonged, a battle to find his identity that he thought was finally won. And now, this happened.

"We're going to start over," Angeline said. "Caleb, this is your cousin, Anna."

Chapter Sixteen

Holding the envelope out at arm's length, Uncle Henry said, "Yo' man be sendin' dis here letter."

"Is he alright?" Amanda reacted nervously and Uncle Henry calmed his voice in response.

"Yessum," he stretched the word slowly. "He be goin' ta Jackson is all. Dis here be splainin' ebryting."

"Thank you," she responded mechanically as she turned quickly away from him and tore open the envelope.

Dear Amanda,

Please don't be worried. I'm fine. I met here in Grenada with Fly and also with Sanford's attorney, a man name Claiborne Barr. He offered you five-thousand dollars for the plantation. Fly advises you to take it and says you have no chance in court. But, if they were so sure of that why would they seem so anxious to get it settled quickly? I think they're both under the same blanket and that there's more to it than we know. Anyway, I refused and told them you needed time to think it over.

Then, as luck would have it, Henry put me on to a prominent Negro gentleman here who has agreed to help us and I am accompanying him by rail to Jackson to engage our own attorney to look into this whole thing. We can't trust Fly. I'm sure of that.

I'll be back in two days. Send Henry to Grenada to meet me. I know it would be futile to suggest that you stay out of it until I get back. Hopefully you'll at least be very careful. Keep a close eye on Anna, she's young...

"Anna!" she startled at the thought, only just then realizing how long her granddaughter had been gone. She ran to the veranda and called out for her in every direction. "Anna!" she screamed and then peered out into the darkness, listening intently, but only a dog barking in the distance responded. "Anna!" she screamed again and more dogs joined the mocking chorus.

For a few seconds she felt completely alone and helpless, with no one near her that she could turn to. How important Thomas was to her at that moment could not be overstated. The uncontrollable image of her mother dying alone and the guilt she carried rose again to magnify her anguish. It came from nowhere, triggered by the most unexpected and unknown things. She looked again at the note, now barely legible in the fading light flickering out through the open doorway and was momentarily comforted to know that she was not alone.

...Your devoted husband,
Tom

"She'll be alright," a clear strong voice broke through from behind her and Amanda turned as the woman added, "She's with Angeline and Caleb. They'll be home soon."

"Lula, you came back!" Amanda responded moving instantly to her primary purpose.

"This is my home," Lula replied caustically.

"Caleb's your son isn't he?" Amanda forced the issue forward. "And my brother was his father, wasn't he?"

"Why is it so important to you?" Lula reacted aggressively. "Do you think we're going to end up as one happy family? Is that what you think?"

At the risk of letting the encounter degenerate into a dispute, Amanda said firmly, "I came here to do what's right by your son," and then in a needlessly nasty tone, "something you apparently don't care about."

Lula tightened her lips and glared. "Don't you dare lecture me about caring for my son."

Amanda pushed harder. "I'm not lecturing you... Mrs. Olmstead." She said the name with emphasis and stinging effect. "I'm just trying to understand you. Don't you want Caleb to get his rightful inheritance?"

Lula had never been called that by a White person before and the words stirred an almost tormenting mix of memories and emotions. "Let it go, please... don't put him in the middle of this," she almost pleaded. Amanda noticed the change of tone, a complete reversal of it in fact, and was taken back. She didn't respond and Lula went on. "My son is Black, Mrs. Hamrick, and he finally knows it. He hasn't lived at Grassy Water for over five years. Don't try to drag him back where he doesn't fit. Do what you want with this place, but please leave us out of it."

"But it's his land!" Amanda responded loudly.

"He doesn't want it," Lula shot back.

Amanda was bewildered and frustrated, but was beginning to sense the social and cultural complexities she was encountering and changed tack. "It's not only Caleb. What will you do? Where will you go?"

"I'll be alright; don't worry about me."

Amanda wasn't deterred. "Why shouldn't you and your son at least have the proceeds from the sale of the land? Let me at least give you the money." When Lula didn't answer Amanda knew she had finally made a little progress and decided not to push her luck. "Where are they?"

Lula, too, was happy to back away. "Angeline took her to meet Caleb. They should be right along," she said and then in a very soft and sincere tone added, "Your granddaughter is a very sweet girl. You should be very proud of her."

"Yes, Lula, yes... we are... very proud." Amanda was thankful that the cloud was lifting and for the first time she began to see the woman in front of her and somehow out of it all began to understand her. "I'm told there's a wedding in the wings."

The two women smiled, each knowing that the other only wanted what was best and that somehow a way would be found.

As the two men climbed into the Senator's private Pullman parlor car, Bruce said, "value in relation to bulk, that's the key. It is generally prohibitive to move farm product over roads, even good roads. Canals and rivers did the job and now railroads are penetrating the areas that had no good water routes, opening up a lot of new land to production."

"Bulk to value ratio," Thomas repeated, vaguely remembering how Samuel came to be in Mississippi in the first place. "That's why so much corn is turned into swine," he mused. "It can be brought to market on the hoof. Pickled or salted and put into barrels, its bulk to value ratio, as they say, is greatly improved."

"Not only corn to pork, Hamrick, but corn to whiskey as well," Bruce said with a chuckle as he took a bottle of Kentucky Bourbon and two glasses from his little portable liquor cabinet and the two men settled back into the overstuffed swivel loungers to relax while waiting for the train to depart.

"Tell me, Mr. Bruce, speaking of railroads, what do you think of the Illinois Central?"

"How do you mean?" Bruce asked as he generously poured the corn whiskey into Thomas's glass.

"As an investment, I mean."

"In common stock?"

"I met a man recently who told me that railroad investment was really about land speculation," Thomas replied smiling. "What do you think of that?"

"Well, yes that's partly true. There's no doubt that the really big killings are made in land sales. But, there's a lot of risk there too, my friend," Bruce answered a bit evasively. "What exactly did you have in mind?"

Thomas sensed that he had stumbled upon a man with vast experience both in business and government, a man who could tell him things that would not only benefit his son, but also might provide clues to solve the more immediate mystery concerning his brother-in-law's estate. "My son asked me to learn what I could, while I was down here, about the future plans of the Illinois Central.

Apparently he's looking for a place to put some money and he believes they have a southern strategy of some sort and if he could better understand it he might..."

"Get ahead of the curve... sure, I understand..." Bruce interrupted and Thomas sat back, sipped his whiskey and listened. "During the war the direction of eastbound shipping in the Midwest changed from starting south down the Mississippi and out at New Orleans to going north through Chicago and the lakes and then on to the eastern seaboard. So in a way the war made the Illinois Central what it is today.

But, gradually after the war other rail lines penetrated in from the East. The Pennsylvania Central and the New York Central laid track right across Illinois. Even the Baltimore and Ohio came west, I believe. So the I.C. found itself gradually being squeezed and started to look south again. But, they're not the only ones with that idea, so there is a race going on, so to speak, to connect the northeast markets directly with the gulf by rail."

"That's very interesting," Thomas replied, "an all-rail route to bypass the Mississippi and Ohio River system entirely."

"Exactly, now when you remember that all the southbound traffic on the lower Mississippi was flowing out at New Orleans you begin to see the other end of the equation."

"New Orleans?" Thomas asked.

"No, not New Orleans, Mr. Hamrick... Mobile, Alabama. Mobile is the natural enemy of New Orleans, commercially that is, good port, but no link to the heartland. An all-rail route connecting the northeast and Mobile, that's what it's all about. It solves both problems."

"An alliance made in heaven you might say," Thomas offered.

"Or hell, Mr. Hamrick, depending on your perspective, because, remember, the I.C. is not the only one in the game," Bruce cautioned.

Thomas finished his sentence for him. "...and a lot of track still has to be put down."

"Voila, my friend," the Senator replied warming more and more to the conversation. "You know this is real bourbon whiskey, made in Kentucky," he digressed offering to replenish Thomas's drink. "There's a lot of Illinois and Tennessee corn calling itself bourbon you know. But this is the real deal."

Thomas covered the top of his glass with his hand to politely decline. He wasn't interested in discussing the nuances of corn whiskey and didn't respond, gently nudging Bruce back to his narration.

"Everybody knew the key to building railroads through the wilderness would be getting federal land grants and trying to get them was almost an obsession for Illinois politicians, especially Stephen Douglas who made a career out of it. But, getting a direct land grant was not easy because of so much opposition." Bruce noticed Thomas nod his agreement and added, "I'm sure you New Englanders always felt that this was something of a fairness issue with special interests cashing in so to speak from the sale of public lands."

"I always thought it was unconstitutional to boot," Thomas replied quickly. "The federal government has no business building railroads and, let's face it, that's what this was all about."

"The political opposition to it in Congress was a more immediate problem," Bruce corrected. "Douglas understood that as long as it was only benefiting Illinois his scheme would never get enough votes in the Senate. So, to roll the log, he expanded the giveaway to include lands in other states too. It was passed in 1850 and was the start of the big railroad land bonanza we've got now."

"There's no question that land giveaways are popular all across the South."

"And it's no wonder, especially after the war, with Dixie devastated and most of the railroads smashed and abandoned. They just couldn't get back on their feet without some serious rebuilding and they couldn't do that without northern investment capital and nothing can pull that in better than free government land!"

"I can see it all in theory," Thomas commented and then asked, "but how does it play out specifically, here in Mississippi I mean?"

"Well, keep in mind that this idea to connect the gulf with the northeast goes back to before the war and most of the southern section had already been built. It's the Mobile and Ohio line that runs up from the gulf well east of the I.C. tracks that come down through Grenada. If the M&O could be connected to the Penn Central say..."

"So you're saying that the I.C. might get squeezed out again?"

"Exactly! They'll fight like hell to block any north-south railroad building scheme to the east of them. It's going to be about securing the strategic parcels of land to control key right-of-ways and river crossings."

Thomas's mind was racing ahead as he relentlessly pursued his second motive. "And this new railroad line would have to cross the Yalobusha, wouldn't it?"

"More than likely, Hamrick. You just get a map and find the best route from the big rail hub at Grand Junction, Tennessee and run your finger on down to West Point Mississippi and see where it takes you. It would be pretty tough to miss the Yalobusha. I'd say some place pretty close to where you're sitting right now and they sure as hell couldn't use the bridge at Grenada."

"Why West Point?" Thomas questioned.

"Because that's where the M&O ends!"

The car lurched forward and Thomas watched the last of the whiskey swirl in the bottom of his glass thinking he had begun to unravel the puzzle. He looked down at the river below and saw it dotted with boats and barges stretching off to the west where it flowed into the Yazoo and disappeared. Then he looked to the east and saw it winding its lonely way into the wilderness.

As the train rolled slowly up and over the bridge, Thomas noticed a small steamboat pass under them in the water below. He stood up and crossed to the opposite side of the car, pulling back the heavy drapes that covered the big plate glass window. As the boat moved up the river away from them the name "Essayons" came clearly into view across the stern.

"That boat there," he blurted out to Bruce who had joined him at the window, "Do you see it there? That must be the boat that was up near Grassy Water a few days ago."

"Essayons," Bruce remarked. "Sure, they're in the river quite often. That's a survey boat, army engineers. Essayons is their motto; it's on all their boats. They're checking the channel, clearing snags, mapping the bottom. The Yalobusha is navigable all the way up to Grenada, it's they're job to keep it that way."

"But they were way up past Grenada," Thomas remarked suspiciously. "You said mapping the bottom. Could they have been surveying a site for bridge construction?"

"I don't see any reason for them to be that far up. The water must already be very low. I'm surprised that they didn't go aground themselves."

"How would I find out?"

"The nearest home port of The United States Army Engineers is in Vicksburg. They'll tell you... Unless it's a military secret," he added, smiling and raising his eyebrows.

Suddenly barking dogs caught their attention and heavy footsteps on the veranda caused Lula to say routinely, "This must be them now." But, then a strong businesslike knock confused her. "That door is never locked," she remarked with a quizzical look and the two women walked quickly through the front hallway to the entrance.

"Are you Mattie Pritchard?" the big man said in a low menacing tone from the shadows.

Lula recognized the county sheriff although she had never formally met him. Everybody recognized the sheriff. Her eyes quickly scanned the front yard and she saw two other men still sitting in their saddles. "How can I help you?" she responded with a nod.

"May I come in? I have something important to say to you."

Amanda was disturbed by the sheriff's tone and worried that something had happened to Anna, but she said nothing. Lula led the sheriff into the front parlor and offered him a chair, but he refused.

"I have here an order for the eviction of Mattie Prichard and all other colored persons residing in any and all of the houses, cabins and other buildings on this plantation." The sheriff handed Lula a paper signed by the lawyer, Graham Fly. The two women read the document and Amanda interrupted.

"This is not a court-ordered eviction."

"Who are you madam?" the sheriff responded.

"My name is Amanda Hamrick. This was my brother's plantation and I am the beneficiary of his will. This land belongs to me, not to Mr. Fly. He has no authority to evict anyone from here."

"That's not true, madam," the sheriff responded. "Mr. Fly is the executor of the will and until it is probated he has paramount title over the property and the power to order her off, which he is doing." He then turned to Lula and asked again. "You are Mattie Pritchard are you not?"

Lula nodded knowingly. For her this was not unexpected. She had a lifetime of experience with the same-old-same-old and was stoically resigned to let it go. "There's no problem, sheriff," she said softly, "I will leave in the morning."

"You most certainly will not!" Amanda declared.

The sheriff tried to avoid a confrontation and said. "It's not necessary that you go that soon. You have ten days to vacate the property."

Amanda found herself fighting on two fronts, but was unwilling to yield. "What is the meaning of this, sheriff? Surely there is no need for this."

"The property is to be sold and must be cleared of all encumbrances."

"Encumbrances! Is that what she is... an encumbrance?" Amanda was incensed. She pulled the paper from Lula's hand and tore it in two. "This is not legal. It can't be. You're just trying to intimidate us," she challenged. "Mattie Prich... Mrs. Olmstead is not going anywhere." She finished assertively hoping that Lula would not contradict her and when she stepped silently forward both women stood shoulder to shoulder and knew that they had forged an alliance.

"This is a title-holder's eviction. It is indeed legal and I strongly advise you to obey it. If Mr. Fly is forced to get a court-ordered eviction he will not hesitate to do so and he wants you informed that if that becomes necessary he will prosecute you for trespass."

Both women were frightened, but they stood their ground. "Good day, sheriff," Amanda declared, opening the door.

Chapter Seventeen

As the train rolled slowly over the Yalobusha bridge, the loud metallic clanking of the heavy door slamming at the end of the car caught their attention. They turned to see two burly mustachioed men dressed in loose fitting tweed sack suits and bowler hats walking slowly through the car, obviously looking for something or someone. They nodded, but said nothing as they passed.

"Ever since the big railroad strikes in 1877, the Pinkerton goons have been all over these trains," Bruce commented after the two intruders exited at the far end of the car.

"Pinkerton, huh," Thomas remarked with some interest, remembering the land office clerk's remark that Pinkerton men had recently inquired about Grassy Water.

"They're nothing but a pack of cutthroats and assassins," Bruce cautioned.

"What do you think they're up to?" Thomas asked.

Bruce shrugged his shoulders. "Most of the railroads have them on retainer I know. They get a blank ticket to ride, supposedly incognito, but, as you can plainly see, they can be as easy to spot as a skunk at the picnic."

"It looked to me like they were searching for someone."

"They patrol the trains, snooping around and asking questions, trying to sniff out trouble, usually labor trouble."

"So you think that's it?"

"I don't know, Hamrick. You know they're supposed to fight crime, but it seems like their most important job is to frighten workers. This country is going to explode if it keeps up. You can't just go on cracking heads..." Bruce seemed very concerned about the labor violence that was beginning to sweep the country and went on for several minutes about it as the train slowly began to gain speed. "Since the big strike a few years back there's been a low grade war on between the workers and their bosses and it isn't going to just go away until something is done. And, I'll tell you something else. If the poor Whites ever figure out that they're in the same pit with the poor Blacks there'll be a revolution in this country."

"But, do you really think strikes and riots will solve anything?" Thomas asked as much out of courtesy as conviction.

"Well... in a word, Mr. Hamrick, yes. What else is there? The union is all the working man has. You can be damned sure the law won't protect them. The working man hasn't got a chance. You're a businessman, Hamrick, have you ever seen it this bad? These tycoons are gobbling up everything; big corporations are out of control. This country's gone cock-eyed. It's got to be brought to balance."

Thomas could see Bruce's emotional involvement and politely tried to further the conversation as best he could, but was not well versed or particularly concerned with the national politics of the moment. "My son tells me that Rockefeller is putting together some sort of trust organization to create a legal monopoly in oil refining."

"That's just what I mean, Hamrick," Bruce shot back; "they'll stop at nothing until they get what they want... everything! Rockefeller, Vanderbilt, Carnegie, the whole rotten pack of them, they really do think they're the favored few of God."

"What do you propose be done about it?" Hamrick asked, politely listening.

"I don't know; it'll take the federal government to straighten it out that's for sure. But, meantime their goons will keep trying to beat the working man down."

"I guess I never really thought about Pinkerton like that before."

"They're a private rich man's police force for God's sake. It shouldn't be allowed. It's usurping the sovereignty of the states. Next thing you know these bastards will be raising their own militias like Chinese warlords."

By the time Caleb, Angeline and Anna reached the big house, the mothers had reached an unspoken accord. One way or the other the question of what to do with Grassy Water would, of course, be decided by Caleb and Angeline, but, as all mothers knew, that decision needed to be nudged in the right direction. It had been the way of parents for all time, letting go of their children always proved to be the toughest task of all.

But, as with most parents, they were undaunted. They talked the candles down. They told him about the lawyer in Jackson and how they wanted him to fight for his rightful inheritance, but he was pessimistic and unimpressed. "You're an Olmstead!" Amanda reminded him, "and Grassy Water is your land."

"The cards are stacked against me," he replied. "Besides, this land is old," he said, "and worn out."

He wanted to buy new land, to own it outright in his real name, his mother's name, her slave name, Pritchard. His mother reminded him that he had no money and would be heavily mortgaged and in debt. He answered with all the naïve bravado of youth, "It doesn't matter; I'll find a way..."

Thomas began. "I understand, Mr. Chambers, that you are the first African American to be admitted to the bar in Mississippi,"

"No, I'm afraid that distinction goes to Mr. James Henry Piles, more than a decade ago," the young lawyer responded as the two men shook hands. "How can I help you, Mr. Hamrick?"

For the next hour Thomas carefully recounted everything he could remember about the problem. Chambers said nothing, but seemed interested in every detail no matter how insignificant it appeared at first to be.

"And you say that your brother-in-law was married to a Black woman, and that her son is the legitimate issue of that marriage?"

"Yes."

"And the widow, is she still living at the plantation?"

"Yes."

"You do realize that interracial marriage is now illegal in Mississippi?" Chambers added leaning forward to emphasize the import of his words. "It's miscegenation; the new state code calls such a marriage incestuous and void and threatens stiff fines and prison terms."

Thomas nodded and said sarcastically, "Will that be a problem?"

They looked at each other and laughed. "It won't help," Chambers responded still smiling. "But, I think I have an idea that could buy us some time at least." He turned to the bookcases that lined the wall behind him and for a few seconds fumbled through several volumes. Thomas strained to see the titles on the spines, but couldn't make out much. "Do you know what dower is, Mr. Hamrick?"

Thomas replied that he wasn't sure and the lawyer explained. "Dower is the right of a widow not to be left destitute after her husband dies. Women have no independent property rights in this country, Mr. Hamrick. Everything legally belongs to the husband. It's outrageous, but true. So the law protects widows by what's called the rights of dower and this right takes precedence over everything."

"Well, what does that mean, exactly?" Thomas asked sensing in the lawyer's tone that there was great significance in this idea.

"It means that she can't be deprived of her home."

"But, there is a contract, as I told you, that stipulates..."

"Yes, I know," Chambers interrupted. "But, the law does not allow a husband to enter any agreement that would deprive his widow of dower. So even if the contract is valid it can't be enforced until after her death."

"So all we need to do is prove that they were married?" Thomas frowned and asked somewhat in disbelief.

"Yes... or lived together in common law bond."

"What about her risk of prison for miscegenation? It seems like by proving they were married we jump from the frying pan into the fire!"

"It's a real risk right now here in Mississippi," Chambers conceded.

There didn't seem to be many options open and Thomas wanted to think this one through carefully. "How would we proceed?"

"First the widow must make a formal demand of dower and serve it on the heirs of the estate, that being your wife, Mr. Hamrick." Chambers chuckled at the ironic neatness of it. "This is called a Writ of Dower. Normally the widow will ask for one-third of the land, which is technically called dower by metes and bounds. She could ask for dower by rents and profits which would allow the estate to be sold in order to provide her with an income, but we want to preserve the estate and give ourselves time to sort it all out."

"And it's Amanda's choice?" Thomas asked rhetorically beginning to warm to the artful scheme.

"Indeed it is," Chambers said smiling. "Mrs. Hamrick should not oppose the granting of dower by metes and bounds and in that way the land cannot be sold before the widow's death, unless it can be shown that it can be equitably divided into thirds and, since, as you say, there is only one suitable landing on the river there is no way to divide the land fairly that way."

"And then what?"

"Her claim is validated by an appointed commission. It's routine. We then petition the court to grant it and your wife will agree to the terms. This case will go to the Court of Chancery, possibly here in Jackson, but probably in Grenada and will almost certainly succeed against any challenge from an ancillary contract. At least it will buy time."

"It can't be that simple," Thomas responded. "What's the worse case scenario?"

"It will undoubtedly immediately generate a challenge from the other side to dismiss the widow's claim to dower on the grounds that she is not legally his wife."

"Will that work?"

Chambers just tilted his head and sighed. "Well, we'd defend on the grounds that the marriage was legal when it was entered into even though it isn't legal today. Mississippi repealed the first ban on interracial marriage in 1870 and after that they were legally married." He paused to reflect and again added with a sigh,

"But, the son was born years earlier, proving that they were intimate together illegally long before. This is clearly going to be a problem."

"And what exactly are they likely to do?"

"They will try to pressure and intimidate us by asking that criminal charges be brought against her..."

Thomas finished the sentence for him, "which could send the woman to prison."

They sat quietly for a few minutes to digest the dangers that could lie ahead. Thomas spoke first. "Of course, it will be completely up to her."

"Yes, most assuredly," the lawyer answered.

"Will you come to Grenada and explain it all to her?"

"Yes, as soon as I can."

"Thank you, Mr. Chambers," Thomas said opening his wallet. "I'm happy that we at least have a plan. Let me offer you a cash retainer."

"That won't be necessary, Mr. Hamrick. Let's wait to see how this plays out, shall we?"

"However it plays out, sir, I'm sure your fee will be well earned."

As he stood to leave, Thomas remembered something else. "You're a Mississippi man, Mr. Chambers, are you not?"

"Yes sir, I am, born and bred as they say."

"Then there may be one more thing you can help me with..." Thomas told the young attorney about his suspicion that Grassy Water was much more valuable than they had been led to believe. "As of now the Illinois Central line has the gulf route all to itself. But there is talk of a plan for a competing line coming down from Tennessee that will go east of the IC tracks to tie in to the M&O at West Point, Mississippi. This line needs to get over the Yalobusha. I've looked at the maps, Mr. Chambers and Samuel's landing seems like a perfect place to build a bridge."

"You realize of course," Chambers asked rhetorically, "if this is true then this crossing could quickly become the hub of a boom town and land values in the whole area would skyrocket!" The lawyer paused briefly and added. "But, beyond looking at maps, what makes you think that the bridge would be at that particular spot?"

"There was an army boat up and down the river recently surveying the bottom right there where the plantation ferry crosses."

Chambers gestured for Thomas to sit down again and said, "Most of the new railroad speculation has been up in the Yazoo. I know that the Louisville, New Orleans & Texas Railway, is planning to run a line up to Memphis from New Orleans via Vicksburg, but that's well west of where you are. Both IC lines from Grand Junction and from Memphis cross the Yalobusha via the bridge at Grenada. I haven't heard of any scheme to go east of them."

"I was told by a very reliable source that a new road down is in the works."

"Well... it could be. It's certainly worth looking into. You said the army engineers were in the river?"

"Last week they were right up at the plantation and just today I saw them going back upstream past Grenada," Thomas responded.

"You know, that would make sense since these railroad schemes now involve the granting of government land. If there is a plan in the works, the army engineers would no doubt be asked by Congress to make a report on feasibility. There doesn't seem to be any other explanation for them to be up there."

"It could be a game changer wouldn't you say?" Thomas asked.

"Indeed it could, Mr. Hamrick," the lawyer responded. "I know someone who may be able to help us. I'll go to Vicksburg before I come up to see Mrs. Olmstead. I'll find out what's going on."

His mother spoke in a commanding tone that left no room for discussion. "It's too late for you to go back; it's out of the question. You'll both stay here tonight."

Caleb smiled and caught Angeline's eye. He knew she was still upset from before and he saw his chance to talk with her alone. From her expression he knew she understood.

Later, after the house was quiet she slipped out onto the veranda where she found him waiting in the loveseat swing. It was an oversized and overstuffed couch piled with pillows and suspended by two heavy chains from the rafters above. In recent weeks they had spent countless hours snuggled together in it talking and dreaming of their future life together. A future that seemed so simple then was now suddenly so terribly complicated.

There was a short length of rope tied to the railing and Caleb stretched his arm to reach it and tug them into a gentle rocking sway.

"Not too hard, Cal, it'll squeak," Angeline cautioned in a loud whisper as she burrowed her shoulder under his arm, kicked off her slippers and tucked her feet under the heavy pillows. He pressed his chin gently against the top of her head and for a long time they just sat there slowly rocking, listening to the tree frogs and cicadas, watching the fireflies and the clouds cross the moon. He gradually began to believe that everything was forgiven and forgotten, but he was about to discover that she was still troubled.

"Why do you have to argue with her," Angeline began. "She's frightened. Can't you see that?"

"She doesn't have to butt-in. This is our life, Angie, not hers. I want us to have it our way."

"You mean your way, I think. There's no reason why you have to be so pigheaded."

"Wake up, Angie. Everything is changed now. This is Jim Crow time now. We can do the fetchin' and the totin' and that's ..."

Angeline pulled herself upright and stiffened her back, turned her head toward him and glared. "And just what do you know about fetchin' and totin'? Listen to yourself. Your mother was the slave not you. She suffered her whole life, all for you. She would give her life for your future happiness and you need to shut up and show some respect."

Although he understood, Caleb could not accept the idea of staying and pretending to be a gentleman farmer at Grassy Water. He couldn't live that nether life, half Black and half White any more. He had to move on, up the country to somewhere else, anywhere else, where he could be his own man and not ever have to feel second-class or look over his shoulder. Angeline didn't yet fully understand that about him, but she was learning.

"I love you, Angie," he said turning toward her. She didn't see the moisture in his eyes, but heard his shaking voice. Then he said it again in a plaintive way that she couldn't ignore "I love you, Angie."

"Please, Caleb it's not about that..." she began, but he interrupted.

"I want us to be together and to be happy, that's all ..."

She pressed her fingers against his mouth to stop him and then pulled her lips up to his; but she felt aloofness in the kiss, opened her eyes and saw him staring into the distance. She pulled her head back, but not knowing what he was thinking, or what to say, she sat silently looking at him.

It was true that he had never been a slave, but he felt like one, he was enslaved in spirit if not in body; his mind was flooded with images of it, like a voice in his head that he couldn't escape. It vexed him night and day.

His color and his features were marked by his mixed racial parentage, most everyone called him a Mulatto. To many that would have been a good thing, but to him it was maddening because he knew in the end it only trumpeted his inferior status; he was Black and would always be Black.

And what did that mean, to be Black when all a Black man could do was follow the ways of White men, imitate them, try to talk like them, dress like them, act like them, while always needing to go a step further, to be whiter than the Whites themselves and yet knowing that it would never be good enough to get beyond the service door, to shine the shoes and light the cigars. It was a taunting torment to know that the only way to beat them was to be just like them. To succeed in their world meant playing by their rules. Work hard and make money; that's how a man rises in status and respect. This was what drove him; it was fast becoming his creed.

He was startled and a little perplexed when she abruptly pulled away. "What's wrong Angie? You will go with me?" he asked, for the first time a little frightened that he wasn't sure of the answer. "You said you would."

"Stop it, Cal," she responded tersely. "You know I will. I'll go anywhere with you. You must know that by now."

He lapsed into a familiar refrain. "There's land opening up north of here and in the delta. It's rich virgin land. The railroads are changing everything, don't you see?" She had heard it all a thousand times. And now she finally knew that he wasn't being pulled by the vision of a far away paradise, but being pushed by the demons behind him.

"You're running away!" she confronted him, justifiably in her mind even if a little cruelly.

"I'm not running away from anything. I just want a new deal, Angie. The deck is stacked. We'd be stupid to stay here; we've got no chance here."

"Where do you think you'll go that Jim Crow won't be there right on your heels?"

"Anywhere where Whites don't own everything and control everything."

Angeline was brutally blunt, "And where's that, Caleb? You can't outrun Jim Crow; you've got to kill him."

There it was again... the choice.

Chapter Eighteen

Thomas had a Pullman parlor ticket, but decided to ride in first class for the trip back to Grenada. He was surprised to find that the car was not segregated by race. Although there were two Negro women seated in it, there was no effort made to move them. Some of the White passengers were visibly annoyed and he could make out the conductor commenting that there was only one first class car on the train and that the railroad could not afford to pull a second one for so few Black passengers. Forcing the women, who had bought first class tickets, to ride in second class could lead to a lawsuit that the railroad was not willing to risk. His answer failed to satisfy some.

The incident was ignored by the two ladies, but became the topic of discussion among White passengers all across the crowded car. Thomas placed his hat on the empty seat beside him. Hoping that no one would sit there, he closed his eyes and listened to the conversation in the seat behind him.

"It's not practical, that's all. What happens when Negro prisoners are transported to jail by a White sheriff or when a sick White passenger is traveling with a Negro nurse? It won't work, that's all."

"Maybe not, but both Blacks and Whites want to separate the races and by God they will do it no matter what the federal government says. Tennessee has a law now requiring railroads to have separate cars."

"But them trains travel into states that have no such law. Ya caint have a person changin' railroad cars, back an' forth, evera time the train crosses a state line. This here Mississippi Central is a good example. Since we are obliged to comply with what they're callin'

Tennessee's separate but equal practice, segregation gets pushed right down here into Mississippi, which as yet has no official law requirin' it and no law against it. We're in a kinda Jim Crow... lim...bo, ya might say."

"They're already feeling the pressure down in Jackson to find a way to stop the lawsuits coming from Blacks that say it's just plain wrong."

"Na, it ain't ouah darkies that don't wan' it; it's them fancy pants Yankee lawyers comin' here to start trouble. The Blacks wanna be with they own kine jus' like the Whites. People is all da same."

"The railroads will have to segregate the car, that's all. Public pressure will force them to."

"But, now that the Yankees already got control of the Mississippi Central and are talkin' 'bout buyin' up more, who knows what we'll end up gettin'."

"That's why we need state laws requiring segregation."

"We'll have ta keep ouah eye on what happens up there in Tennessee."

"Well, we'll find out soon enough. The Tennessee-way is before the Supreme Court right now and the whole South is waiting for it to be resolved. This is a big, big issue. I mean does the federal government have the power to force private citizens to associate with certain people against their will."

"And ya say we're 'bout to get word 'bout it?"

"They're hearing it right now. If Tennessee Jim Crow gets upheld you'll see White's-only signs sweep across the South."

"Amen, brother."

Thomas was falling asleep; he thought he heard a third voice enter the conversation, but he was slowly losing contact. The rhythmic clanking of the wheels as they hit the little bump between sections of track blended hypnotically with the drone of voices until the world was quiet.

Thomas had no idea how long he had slept when he woke to see his hat propped over his knee and a man sitting beside him. "Good morning, Mr. Hamrick," the man said softly with a smile and Thomas recognized him immediately to be one of the Pinkerton men they had seen earlier.

"Good morning, Mr. ...?

"Dumphy, my name is Roger Dumphy; how do you do."

"And, if I may ask, Mr. Dumphy, how do you know who I am?"

"I traced your Pullman reservation and when you weren't in your parlor-car seat the conductor found you for me."

The conversation quickly took on an abrasive nearly hostile tone. "And why would you go through all that trouble, Mr. Dumphy, do you take me for a union organizer?"

"And why would I do that?"

"You're a Pinkerton man aren't you?"

"Well, well, Mr. Hamrick," Dumphy responded jovially, "it seems we're both detectives. No, this has nothing to do with that."

"What then?"

"I understand that you are looking for Jean Gareau."

"Now how did you come to that conclusion?"

"Please, Hamrick, lets not waste each other's time," Dumphy reacted in a suddenly serious tone. "I can help you. You went to the land office in Grenada and asked about Gareau. You also spoke to several others about your desire to locate him. You haven't exactly been hiding it now have you?"

Thomas made no effort to mask his dislike for Dumphy yet he knew that the man might be useful and wanted to go on. "Why would that interest you, Mr. Dumphy, do you know where Gareau is?"

"Jean Gareau's name is on our wanted list. Someone is after him and is willing to pay very well to see that he is found." Dumphy paused briefly and then asked, "I trust that's not you, Hamrick?"

"No, it's not me." Thomas responded somewhat puzzled. He paused for a few seconds to collect his thoughts. This piece of information changed everything and added a new element of urgency to the search for Gareau. "Don't you know who the client is?"

"It's confidential, but it has a high priority; there are two men on it full time and every agent is ordered to inquire about him and report any leads."

"With no luck?"

"Not yet, but we'll get him, rest assured of that."

"Assuming that I am looking for this man, and I don't mean him any harm mind you, but suppose I wanted to talk to him, how could you help me?"

"Look... Hamrick, I don't care who finds Gareau, but sooner or later someone will. And I don't care what happens to him. If you want to slit his throat that's fine with me. I don't ask any questions. I just do my job and keep my mouth shut."

"What job are you referring to?" Thomas shot back. "Just what do you want, Dumphy?"

"Money of course! I can keep an eye on this for you, inside Pinkerton and when one of our agents locates him I can tip you off about where he is and you can get to him first."

"And how much did you have in mind?"

"One-hundred dollars!"

"That's a lot of money, Mr. Dumphy." It was an impulse and it could have been a simple scam, but it was the best lead Thomas had and Dumphy seemed just slippery enough to be double dealing his own employer. "I'll give you twenty dollars now and the rest when you tell me where I can find Gareau."

"Done!"

"You have a few days, maybe a week, before it's too late. I have a room at the Planter's Hotel in Grenada. Leave word there."

Angeline was worried. The wedding was upon her and now suddenly she saw a side of him she had never seen before, a bitter, angry and cynical side. This was the man she loved and she knew he loved her, but there was much more that she needed to know. They sat in the swing and talked until they were tired and sleepy; or better he talked and she mostly listened.

"Slavery has ended, but anyone can see that the Black man is slowly being driven down into another kind of bondage. It's subsistence slavery where he is kept forever poor to provide cheap labor."

"But it's not... slavery, Cal. People are free to negotiate their own wages, change jobs..."

"It might as well be. It's the infernal labor contract system. It's just another kind of slavery. And they use the laws to pull the rope tighter and tighter around our necks. So long as they own all the land they'll have all the power. You either work for the White man or end up in the chain gang."

She was beginning to understand that his quiet rage was rooted in a fundamental feeling of inequality, of being cheated and discriminated against. What good was freedom if he couldn't protect his equality and how long could that freedom endure without it? She wanted him to let it out and she wanted to support him no matter so she encouraged him. "It just doesn't seem right, Cal. Labor is so critical to this way of life that it would seem that the workers would hold the upper hand. I mean after all they can quit."

A look of incredulity that she pretended not to see swept over his face as though proclaiming that only an ignoramus could say such a stupid thing. "They can't quit, Angie," he proclaimed shaking his head. "They try like hell to migrate north where at least the wages are livable, but vagrancy laws make it a crime to quit your job and that lands them in jail where then they get contracted back as cheap convict labor to the same farms they're trying like hell to get away from. Now if that don't beat all!"

This demon definitely had a hold on him and it frightened her a little so she decided to back away and let him vent and lecture her on something she had long practiced pretending not to know anything about.

"But, even with all that, the whole South is leaking labor like a sieve and so they come up with the next scheme to keep us in bondage," he said it with hissing hatred, "share cropping... They started breaking those big worn-out farms up into forty or fifty acre pieces and divvying them up, so a man worked for a part of the crop. It's sad to see so many brothers so happy about putting their money down in a game that they have no hope of winning."

"They have to start somewhere, Cal. They can rent land; if they work hard..."

"It's all the same shit, don't you see? It's the White man's scam and the Black man's going to pay the price. Where do you think he gets the money to buy seed and tools? He borrows it from some White middleman and ends up with debts he can never get out from under. It's bullshit Angie and it will always be bullshit."

"Aren't there other ways to get ahead, Cal? Do you think it's only about money and land?"

"It's usually about land, yes; and it's damn sure always about money. The only ones I see amount to anything own property. If they're Black you've got to go north to find them. Down here we're just mules... we're cheaper than mules... we're donkeys and that's all we'll probably ever be."

"Don't you think education is part of the answer? More and more Blacks are going to colleges and entering the professions."

"And they're all going to be philosophers and poets," he derided with obvious disdain. "I want to own land, a lot of land; I want people to work for me and owe me money, not the other way around and the only place where that can happen is up the country in the new railroad land grants."

"Why can't it happen right here at Grassy Water? You know you're the rightful owner of this place. It's our home, Cal, all of our family and our friends are here. It just seems wrong not to fight for it."

"You aren't listening to me, Angie. We can't win that fight."

"How do you know, Cal?"

It was raining when the train arrived at Grenada station and Thomas was relieved to see Uncle Henry waiting in the hooded one horse buggy. "You must have gotten up early, Uncle," he said smiling as he climbed into the seat beside the old man.

"I waked up bout fi. Jus befo' sunup like usual."

Thomas told Uncle Henry about his need to find Jean Gareau and about the Pinkerton detective, hoping that the old man might know something and was stunned by his response.

"I knows jus' 'bout where he be. Ebrybody know..."

"You know where Gareau is?" Thomas interrupted before the old man had finished

"Shur nuf he be shacked up wit old lady Sally!" Henry replied as though it were the most common of knowledge. Thomas's jaw dropped and the pause drew Henry on. "She be a mixed blood what tuk care a de chilluns fer some White folks up 'roun' here somewhares. Her pappy be nuffin' but po white trash, but Gareau shu did take a shinin' to 'er. Dey bin shackin' up tagether fer a long time. Dey nebber did jump ober da broom fars I know."

“Do you know where to find her, Henry?”

“She got a little place right here down Perry’s Creek a ways. Nebber bin dere my own self... too many skeeters, but I knows whare tis.”

“Who else would know that Gareau might be with this woman, Uncle?”

“Ebrybody know it, ceppin’ dem Pinkertins seem like.”

“Can you bring me there?”

“Dere ain’t no real road, jus’ a rutty track... Dey try ta keep a road, but wit all de mud sometimes deys no a bottom under it.”

“We’ll walk then.”

“You gonna foot it bout fo mile?” He asked.

“If I have to.”

Uncle Henry looked up toward the southern sky where breaks of blue could be seen in the overcast. “Dat rain be coming on de gulf wind... outta de south. Gonna be lettin’ up real soon.”

“When we gits dere we gonna probly fine her, but he be hidin’ in de woods fer shur. You gonna hab ta do some fancy talkin’ ta git ‘im ta come out.”

Angeline began before the door had fully closed. “The dress is so beautiful Aunt Effie, but the train is so long I don’t know how I can carry it.”

“You ain’t spossed ta hole it up by yo self, chile. The trail gonna be so long it’ll take two, maybe three, chilluns to hole it all up and one a de maids will be side ya all da time. You doan lif a finger, chile.”

Angeline helped the old woman lower herself down onto her knees and then stepped up onto the small stool. “Dis gonna hab ta be the las tuck Angeline cause Aunt Effie got no mo tread.”

The final fitting, she thought thankfully to herself as she shifted her weight restlessly from foot to foot, and after this all that remained would be the beading, some flounces and lace frills on the sleeves. She noticed, but never truly appreciated, how carefully Aunt Effie removed the tiny stitches she had so painstakingly put in only days before, to pull in the waist one more time.

To Angeline the endless measuring and fitting was an ordeal, but to Aunt Effie it was in the essence of her frugality and a testament to her patience, but she was running out of silk thread. Mistakes were costly and the fine fabric nearly irreplaceable; and besides any substitute would certainly not match perfectly and everything had to be perfect.

"You gotsta eat. You be fadin' away, chile."

"This should be the last time. There are only a few days more now."

"Oh, you gonna hab some weddin' Angeline, a big beautiful weddin' jus like the White folks usta do in the big house. It'll be so fine. I members dem weddin's... "

Just the mention of slavery drove her doubts back to the surface. Marriage was a frightening moment in any young woman's life, even in good times, and these times were surely not good. They had almost nothing to their name and now he seemed obsessed with the idea of moving north into the back country. She knew he loved her and that eased her mind a bit, but it wasn't enough. She needed to understand him and for the first time the thought arose that maybe this was a mistake! Her heart pounded and she tried to push the thought away by focusing on Aunt Effie's rambling reminiscence.

"...how all de little ones would peek in from de windows ta see da bride an' de weddin' dress an' de long trail. I swore I'd have a dress like dat some day... only dat day nebber come. So Aunt Effie want you ta hab..."

Suddenly she couldn't suffer that stool any longer and without warning stepped down and, to cover her tears, ran to the window.

"What's wrong, chile?" Effie asked as she slowly struggled to her feet. "You sit right here and tell Aunt Effie what's wrong."

"Why is he so angry?" Angeline blurted out between sobs. "He's gotten so bitter and cynical about his life."

"Cause he ain't free."

"The laws make him free and equal," Angeline retorted although she knew well the gap between legal standing and social equality. "He has civil rights, the same as everybody else."

"Look 'roun, girl; Is dat what you see?"

Angeline didn't want to fall back into the same pit that was already burying her and she refocused the question. "I just want to live a quiet life, have children, be happy. Is that too much to ask?"

"Well dat's what he want too"

"But, sometimes he gets so mad, Aunt Effie. It frightens me."

"Deez young Negro mens taday is lost, lots of 'em. Dey wone listen to dere elders no mo'. Dey look at 'em and see slaves who doan talk right and doan know nothin'. Caleb ain't like dat. He be a good man, Angeline. He doan boast and brag and trow his money away like some a deez young bucks ya see struttin' 'roun' and playin' look-at-me. Anger be a bad bad ting. You gottsta help im turn it fer good."

"I just wish I understood him. I thought I did, but now I just don't think I really know him."

"Da Black man ain't no different from da White man. He got a powful pride. He wanna stand up and take comman' a somethin'. Only dere ain't nothin' fer 'em ta take comman' of. Bout the only place a Colored man can get dat is by bein' a preacher. Dere like lords reigning in dere castles. Dere word be sacred wit ebrybody swingin' and swayin' and sayin' amen amen after ebry line dey say. Ebry man want dat. Dat's what Caleb want. Da trouble be dat he know he be in a White man's worl' and he be fraid he cain't get it. But he kin get it. Dat be yo job. You help 'im get it."

"I know he's a good man..." she answered with deep emotional conviction that told Aunt Effie that in the end all would be well, "...and I really love him, but..."

Effie cut her short. "Hush girl; climb back up on yo' stool. New bride always git dem doubts. You be proud a yo' man, dat's all he want."

Chapter Nineteen

Amanda had been waiting on the veranda for hours. She fell in and out of sleep a hundred times it seemed, lulled away by the gentle murmurs of the night only to be jarred awake by any hint that the ferry-crank was turning. She opened her eyes and listened again expecting to hear another owl screech or a cat scream or nothing at all until she dozed away again; but this time the rhythmic scratching of the rusted gear was unmistakable. She stood near the railing and listened as the yawning cable finally fell silent and the heavy ferry raft thumped its dead weight against the mooring post. It was very late and she smiled knowing that he was home at last.

Thomas's body was dead tired from the two-day trip, but his brain was bubbling with excitement at the thought of telling his wife what he had learned and how the mystery was unfolding and about the lawyer's clever plan to frustrate Fly and the others. There was something riveting about it all that made him feel more alive than he had in years. It was as though he didn't want it to end and that to resolve it would be a great loss somehow.

"We found that so-called partner of your brother's, Gareau," he began before she could say anything. "He was hiding in the deep woods right where Uncle Henry said he would be..."

Amanda was so relieved to have her husband home and safe and he seemed so excited that she overlooked his hurried kiss and seeming indifference to her tight embrace. There was a time when this would have bothered her, lingered in her mind, even subverting her thoughts, but not any more. She knew that it had never occurred to him that she was there waiting and worried and that in the end it really didn't matter at all. "Sit down, Tom, before you burst."

"Gareau was frightened and suspicious, but he finally told me everything he knew, or thought he knew, about this business. It's a scam, Mandy. I knew it all along. And we've got a lawyer and a plan."

"Slow down, Tom. Start from the beginning. You went to see the lawyer..."

"Yes, the lawyer, in Jackson, but before that..."

Thomas recounted every detail he thought significant about his meeting with Senator Bruce and how he saw the mysterious boat in the river again. He explained why he began to believe that someone was plotting out a new rail route south right through Grassy Water. "At first I thought it was the Illinois Central, but Bruce and the lawyer in Jackson, Virgil Chambers, they told me that if anything it was probably the reincarnation of an old plan to run a line down to Mobile, Alabama. Now, that road would likely go over the Yalobusha River right about where we're sitting!"

The significance of that was not for a second lost on Amanda and it certainly cast suspicion on Sanford's claim to the land. "Why did you say it was a scam, Tom? What else do you know?"

"Well, it seems this Sanford owns a gambling saloon, some sort of houseboat anchored in the river, a couple of miles below Grenada. Gareau was a regular there and he lost heavily. In the end, to cover his debt, he had to hand over the deed to his land. But, that wasn't the end of it. Apparently when Sanford discovered the possibility that the property was a potential goldmine he hatched the scheme to get control of your brother's side of the river too. That would give him both banks right where the bridge would be built. Everybody knew that Samuel was close to death. That's when they concocted a bogus contract giving Gareau the option to buy the land when your brother died. Only thing was, he needed Gareau to go along with it, which he agreed to do... for a price."

"So, you're sure that the contract is a fake?"

"Oh... it's a fake alright, but proving it won't be easy."

"Well, you said that ..."

"Gareau is scared, Mandy," he interrupted. "He won't come forward. He's on the run. They're after him; he thinks they're trying to kill him and I think he's right."

"Why do you say that, Tom? Who's trying to kill him, Sanford?"

"Who else? I talked to a Pinkerton man on the train. He told me that someone hired them to find Gareau and then tell them where he was..."

"Who hired them?"

"He didn't know, but when I told that to Gareau he turned white as a ghost. He said the original plan was for him to disappear and never come back and that was exactly what he was going to do."

They both sat for a few seconds and said nothing. Then Amanda broke the silence. "What now?"

"It was a neat little scheme until we showed up," Thomas commented, chuckling half to himself, but the significance of it struck Amanda another way.

"You don't think they'll try to kill us do you?"

"No, of course not... that's... no..." he stammered giving some credence to the idea he was summarily dismissing.

"God, Tom... what are we getting ourselves into?"

"We're not getting in Mandy; we're already in. We're trying to get out."

"You said you had a plan. What sort of plan?"

Thomas told her about his meeting in Jackson and about the lawyer's idea to have Mattie-Lou claim the right of dower as a way to block the execution of the contract. It would give them time get some answers and possibly expose the scheme. "That boat was an army engineer's survey. Chambers is going to Vicksburg to find out what it was doing there. He agrees there is a good chance that the whole thing is contrived to get control of the land where they think the river crossing will be."

"But you said we couldn't prove it. If Gareau won't testify how can we stop it?"

"I don't know yet, Mandy. But the first thing we need is time and this claim for dower will get us that. Do you think she'll do it?"

"Honestly, Tom, I have no idea. She's very strong willed and pessimistic about the whole thing, but, I hope in the end she'll see that she has nothing to lose and..."

"That's where you're wrong," Thomas interrupted and went on to tell her about the Mississippi miscegenation laws and the threat of prison that would hang over her head should she admit to having married a White man.

"Would they do that?"

"Chambers thinks they will."

The voice was assertive, practiced and strong and the sound came suddenly from nowhere. "I want you to know that I loved your brother and he loved me."

Amanda looked up from the letters and ledger books that were spread across her brother's desk. She had spent most of the morning back in the business room searching for anything that could better explain her brother's life. For her this had been as much as anything, an opportunity to find out who he was and what he had become, to fill in that huge gap in her life that until now she believed would be forever lost. "I know he did," she answered sympathetically. "I'm so glad you're here. I know so little about him. I need to learn more about him. I so hope he was happy."

"Do you want to see the grave?" she said softly. "I'm going there now."

"Yes... I was going to ask you. Is it here at Grassy Water?"

"We've got a little spot where most of the folks here are laid to rest. That's where he wanted to be."

"I wish I had flowers to bring," Amanda said with a hint of genuine excitement.

Mattie smiled and responded, "You won't need to; you'll see."

The two women walked the few hundred feet to the simple graveyard, out of sight just over the crest of a small rise. The grave markers were mostly plain wooden crosses with awkwardly whittled words of remembrance standing above a sea of golden coreopsis that covered the hillside and swayed away to the horizon on the gentle breeze. The sun was already high in the sky and the heat of the day drove the bees to their labor. Half-hidden among the flowers was his single simple stone.

Suddenly everything was calm and serene. "What a beautiful place," Amanda said, but Mattie's mind was elsewhere.

"I never wanted to marry him. There was no way that I would be seen as anything more than a vamp, but that wasn't true. I never dallied or made eyes at him." It was plain that she had been plagued her whole life by these thoughts.

"You don't have to explain anything to me, Mattie," Amanda made the obligatory half-protest, although she was burning to hear more and in an almost perfect symbiosis Mattie needed to respond.

"They're always trying to explain it like it was unusual or crazy or something. We fell in love, that's all. There's nothing else to it. I could tell the first second I saw him. I knew that as long as I was just his mistress or his concubine as they say, everything would be fine around here. That's the way it was. But, if I married him... well... believe me that would not do."

"You were a slave, Mattie," Amanda said suddenly remembering and realizing. "You're the young woman he bought in the auction," she then added rhetorically. Amanda's words penetrated deeply and pulled the woman back to that auction block in Natchez a half-century before. It was a nightmare she had always tried to forget.

"I saw it in his eyes. I felt the trust in his touch when he took my hand. I always felt safe with him. He was the only White man I wasn't afraid of. But, I could never be more than a fancy girl, and of course, that's what they all called me." Amanda saw the tears well up in Mattie's eyes and the intensity of her struggle to push them back down. Mattie-Lou had learned very early in her life never to waste tears. "He always wanted to marry me, but I knew that would only make it worse."

"But, you did marry him."

"Yes, I did. That was then. But, it's all different now." Amanda asked with her expression and the woman continued. "Nowadays all you hear is about sexual relations between the races and how awful that is. But, it never was sex that anyone objected to. Everybody knows there was plenty of that. It was marriage that they were afraid of because marriage between the races was recognition of equality. That's what they hated. That's the sin we committed."

Amanda was beginning to understand the deeper cultural roots of the problem they faced in securing the estate for Samuel's son. Her mind began streaming and mixing Mattie's words with her own purposeful thought.

"White men never had any problem sleeping with Negro women. The problem they had was in recognizing the babies they got from it..."

What to do with the growing number of Mulatto children of White fathers was a big problem that threatened...

"...For the most part they're the ones who suffer. And there's so many of them now. That's what's bothering my son and all the rest of the mixed bloods..."

If the White fathers recognized the mixed race children it would undermine the very idea of White racial superiority and might ...

"...You northerners don't have the kind of interracial life like we do here in the South. You don't know the first thing about it. Down here Whites know in their heart that the races will mix all on their own. Northerners don't believe that, but it's true. It's inevitable unless it is prevented. That's why the Whites down here are so afraid of it. They can see where it's headed. Every tan face is testament to it. It'll get that way up north too, you wait and see."

"But, you did marry him and it worked out alright, I think."

"It was good that he didn't have any family here. We stayed quiet and never had to live up to other people's ideas about what's what. And like I said, we were in love."

"And you have a son. Don't you want him to inherit his father's name?"

"I don't want to see him lynched, especially over a piece of worn-out land."

"It's not about the land, you know that."

The words rang true in Mattie's mind. She was tired, tired of being quiet and tired of avoiding trouble and most of all she was tired of being pushed around, but it was ingrained in her and was all she knew. "What can I do?"

When Thomas reached the barn Uncle Henry had already harnessed up the horse and was waiting to hitch the carriage. Thomas hadn't yet told him that he would be driving Amanda into Grenada himself, since the little buggy could only carry two.

"Good morning, Henry. Is everything ready?" Thomas's eye swept quickly around the stable and he was impressed by how clean and neat it was. The stalls were wide and airy and well bedded with what looked like some kind of dried moss that he wasn't familiar with. Everything seemed more orderly than he expected, bridles, harnesses, even the dung basket, hanging on pegs, body brushes, water brushes, sponges and hoof pickers laid out on shelves, pitch forks, brooms and shovels neatly put away.

You can tell a lot about a man by the way he keeps his things Thomas thought to himself. But the stable seemed excessive for only two mules and an old mare. There must have been more horses he thought, in better times, before the war maybe.

"Yessur I'se ready ta roll."

"Mrs. Hamrick and I will be going alone today, Uncle." Thomas was well versed in handling a horse and buggy and thought nothing of it, failing to sense the impact this development would have on the old man. "I'll drive the buggy. That won't be a problem," he repeated noticing Henry's blank look.

"But... I wus always de one dat drives."

"There won't be room, Uncle. Just tell me about the mare. I've driven one of these for my whole life. There's nothing to worry about, really." Uncle Henry loved that old horse. But like almost everything else he ever loved it belonged to somebody else. Thomas didn't notice this at first and then asked routinely, "How is she harnessed then."

"Dis ain't no regula hoss. This here be Beulah. She be a mighty paticula lady hoss dat doan pay nobody no mine... ceppin' me. I gotsta ta talk to 'er mos a da time. We goes back a long, long way. I'm da only one eber drives 'er. I doan know if she gonna take to yo'."

"She looks like a gentle well-broken mare, Henry. You don't need to worry; I'm sure I'll be alright."

The thought of seeing his beloved Beulah driven off by a stranger was a heavy burden and Henry struggled to find a way around it. "She like dis here two-part bit. She kin chew on it while she be standin' still. Keeps her hap... yo' gotta be careful though when yo' pull her in cause it be a loose bit and iffin it jumps she might git scart."

"Why don't you tighten the bit?" Thomas asked still unmindful of the emotional bond between the old man and his animal.

"She got a real soff mouth. Doan need no curbs, jus' dis here plain snaffle. So yo' wanna be real gentle-like."

Thomas busied himself feeling the harness and the fit of the collar. Uncle Henry kept talking, searching for some reason why this was not a good idea. "Dat dere be 'er bress strap. Dis be de only one she can wear... She hab ta hab 'er winkers. She git scart iffin she look back an' seed de buggy cumin' on behin' 'er. She doan know no betta." The old man looked for any sign that he might be making headway, but saw none and plowed ahead. "Dis here cruppa come down 'roun' de tail to keep ebryting back. Yo' gotsta keep dis loose or she gonna git mighty mad... an she might kick too."

"Well why don't you add..." Thomas began to suggest, but Henry interrupted assertively and that was very uncharacteristic of him.

"Dats all da ledder she need."

Thomas finally began to comprehend what the old man was really saying. "An doan git in de box 'fore you got de reins... and doan let nobody else git in 'fore you... an doan use da stable at de otel. Go 'roun' to da udder one. An doan let 'em gib 'er any sour hay. Take dis here sack uf oats fer 'er."

Thomas smiled broadly. "What about that?" He asked, motioning with his head to an old two-seat surrey sitting idle next to the barn.

Uncle Henry's eyes lit up. "I kin hab de mooles hitched up in nuffin' flat. Dat way yo' and da misstus can ride in style. Dat shur would make ol' Uncle Henry feel mighty good."

The two-seater might be better Thomas thought. That way maybe Mattie could go with them. It was worth asking her at least.

As Thomas watched Uncle Henry take the bit from Beulah's mouth the thought of Mattie's vulnerability to the miscegenation laws drove the fear that she would be arrested to the surface. Thomas was worried that he might be the cause of further hardship for her and he desperately wanted to avoid that. This was a simple case of fraud. It didn't have to be mixed with the racial struggles of the whole South, but it unavoidably was. Everything was inextricably woven together. You can't escape it, he fretted.

There was something here in this place, something about the people and the culture that he couldn't understand. In fact the puzzle was so great that he even failed to articulate exactly what it was. Life in the South was different from what he knew, but that exact distinction was as yet beyond his capacity to comprehend. This was his first experience in a truly multiracial society. There were so many so-called people of color, of so many categories, Mististoes, Mullatoes, Quadroons, Octoroons, and so many laws and customs meant to control them, where they went, what they did, who they talked to or even fell in love with. Why did we come down here? We don't belong here? His thoughts streamed.

The so-called better citizens of the South like to righteously accuse the people of the North of putting notions of racial equality in the heads of Negro people. But it's the men of the south that as much as trumpet this equality through their widespread sexual liaisons with Negro women. And the proof is in the faces of so many children. Then they try to pretend that it's not so and want to walk away from the truth and make speeches about racial purity and White superiority. It explains why they're so afraid to give an inch and why the mixed race offspring, like Mattie's son, are particularly targeted and why they they're so angry.

There can only be one explanation for this entire obsession with segregation, he finally concluded. It's a façade intended to create elaborate trappings to bolster the myth of Negro inferiority because they know it doesn't really exist.

"Tell me something, Uncle," Thomas said. "Do you like White people?"

"I likes 'em nuf... mos a dem dat is."

Chapter Twenty

Thomas suddenly said, "Pull into the side street there," and Uncle Henry turned the corner and eased the surrey to a stop. Amanda smiled thinking to herself that her granddaughter would have wanted to barge right through the public portico of the Planter's Hotel, but it just wouldn't be proper.

"Tom, you'll escort us in by the lady's entrance," Amanda said assertively.

Since they were not sure how long they would need to be in town and had only one room reserved at the hotel, it would be necessary to register again to get an additional accommodation for Mattie. There was an unmistakable sense of foreboding in not knowing what would happen when they tried to check a Black woman into the hotel and Amanda wanted to be decisive.

There were as yet no official Jim Crow restrictions in Mississippi, but any public place that didn't segregate was shunned by most Whites. It was a surreal scene since much of the hotel staff was Black and only the oddity of perception as to what role a person played made any difference. There was no harm, for example, in Thomas riding beside Uncle Henry in the surrey's front seat, so long the black man was driving. Mattie was likewise welcome at the hotel, but only in the role of a servant, never as a guest or an equal.

"Now, Tom, remember to ask for adjoining rooms and an attached bath." She turned to Mattie and added, "I can't bear one more night with that monstrous washstand and basin."

"I'm not sure they'll have a private convenience," Thomas replied. "It is a luxury you know."

Amanda was nervous; things were coming to a head and she wasn't sure what to expect. She forced herself not to fidget and tried to hide her anxiety by talking. "Perhaps, but try anyway. And as we have no luggage, Tom, you'd better be prepared to pay in advance... and don't bother with the American Plan for meals, I don't think we'll be using the restaurant... and if we do we can order ala carte to be brought up..."

The need to check into the White people's hotel came as a complete surprise to Mattie. This was a major complication and she had very little time to sort it out before the need arose to act. She too was visibly nervous, even Uncle Henry noticed.

Suddenly, as they reached the door, Mattie pulled the bags from Thomas's hands and carried them in.

"What are you doing?" Thomas reacted.

"It's easier this way," Mattie answered marching straight ahead and by pretending to be a family servant she passed hardly noticed through the door and into the lobby.

"I wish we didn't have to play this game?" Amanda remarked pointedly.

"But we do, that's all," Mattie whispered emphatically and then as she refused to allow the porter to take the luggage said distinctly, "I takes care a dis."

Amanda's head snapped around in disbelief, but before she could react Thomas cautioned, "Let her do it her way, Mandy," the look in the woman's eyes convincing him not to trifle with her life any more.

The ladies sat in the public parlor pretending to read the newspaper while Thomas booked the two adjoining rooms and private bath. The desk clerk turned the book back around and read:

Thomas Hamrick, Boston
Mrs. Hamrick,
and maid

"Very good, sir," he mumbled routinely and nodding to the bellboy said, "Show Mr. ...Hamrick... to his rooms."

The ladies watched as Thomas took the key and gave the bellboy a coin in advance. As they walked across the lobby to the main staircase Amanda finally spoke. "Why did you do that?"

"It was for the best. This way we get what we want without any trouble," Mattie replied looking stiffly straight ahead.

"Sometimes it's better to take a stand."

"Yes, sometimes, but not this time."

Thomas expected Virgil Chambers to arrive from Jackson on the 2:15 train. As he walked back and forth along the platform his view alternated from the long empty track rising gently over the bridge and disappearing in the distance to Uncle Henry waiting patiently along the freight dock with the carriage and the mules. As he paced and turned, back and forth, again and again, somehow the two images mixed and merged in his mind.

He thought about the old man and how unassuming and likable he was. He smiled remembering the moonack and how poetic his uneducated and at times almost unintelligible expressions were, that he seemed so happy with so little and seemed to harbor no hatred for anyone. Why isn't he bitter or at least cynical he wondered as he turned to search the distance for any sign of the train. After suffering a lifetime of slavery and the cruel betrayal of freedom he still believed he would get his forty acres and a mule. What will he do now when all of this is settled and Grassy Water is gone? He's all alone in the world and everything will finally look aimless and uncertain, but none of that seems to bother him.

His eye swept across the empty track and then he saw the old man again, laughing and talking to the mules, their ears pricked-up high as though they understood every word and he began to fathom the old man's secret. Uncle Henry was completely of this moment. Right-now was all that mattered and right now he was happy, jollying with his molly mules. He had the gift to know in his heart that life doesn't get any better than that.

Thomas's detachment was suddenly shattered by the sharp whistle of a fast approaching locomotive. That's not right he thought. It's going the wrong way. Then he felt a warm breeze bathe his face as the mail train rolled south through the station.

"You waiting for the Jackson train?" a man asked.

"Yes, sir, I am," Thomas replied.

"She just had to wait for the express to go by. She'll be along in a minute."

Thomas nodded and tried to return to his musing, but he couldn't. The man wouldn't let him.

"That freight yard there used to be busy every day. Now... hell..."

"It'll pick up again," Thomas responded politely, even though he had no interest in meaningless small talk with a man he didn't know and would most likely never see again.

"No... it won't."

Common courtesy forced him to answer. "Why do you say that? There have been ups and downs before."

"It's the Negro problem."

"What is that? The Negro problem..."

"Look over there. That's your boy there ain't it? Why he'll just stand there all day 'til you tell him to move. Good thing there ain't any freight train due and wagons to be unloaded right where he's lollygaggin' around. They're laggards, just naturally lazy. They're killin' the South, and there ain't nothin' nobody kin do about it neither."

Thomas wanted to respond, but thought to himself that it just wasn't worth it. "You'll have to excuse me; I think this is the train now."

The lawyer told Thomas right away that he had been to Vicksburg and had talked to his cousin who was a civilian clerk in the survey office of the army engineers. He learned that the boat they had seen was indeed sent to determine the feasibility of a river crossing at Grassy Water and that they had found the bottom to be solid and suitable for bridge piers of the type needed for a heavy railroad bridge. The report was set for release in a few days.

"That does it then," Thomas exclaimed. "That's what it's all about. They're just trying to get the land. I'm sure it's a scam now."

"Maybe so, but there's more to it," Chambers responded. "I had a hunch and asked my cousin to go back and get a look at the whole file. The army is pretty secretive about these reports since there's so much speculation riding on them."

"They wouldn't falsify something like that would they?"

"No, probably not, but they release results piecemeal and hold the bad news for last and that can create false impressions. And there is bad news. Like I said, the river bed and banks are fine, but the swampy bottoms just south of there are too soft and muddy. They would have to be backfilled for miles to support a track."

"Well where does that leave us?"

"It means that the proposed route through your plantation land has been rejected as not cost effective. But..." Chambers paused for emphasis, "nobody knows it yet. I think we ought to rethink our strategy, after all turnabout is fair play, wouldn't you agree, Mr. Hamrick?"

There's no doubt that Thomas would have agreed had he heard Chamber's remark, but his concentration was co-opted at that very moment by what looked to be some commotion developing around Uncle Henry and the carriage. The two men hurried as fast as Thomas's elderly legs could carry him and reached the scene just as the sheriff was about to take Uncle Henry into custody.

"What are you doing?" Thomas asked trying to place himself between the sheriff and his driver.

"Get down from there," the sheriff commanded.

"What's this all about, sheriff? That man is in my employ. I told him to wait here if that's the problem."

"I'm afraid it's more serious than that, Mr. Hamrick. You are Thomas Hamrick are you not?"

Thomas was puzzled as to how the sheriff could possibly know who he was, but didn't ask. "Tell me what this is all about, sheriff."

"It's about murder!" the sheriff responded with a squint in his eye.

"Murder?"

"We have reason to believe that Jean Gareau has been killed, murdered, last night or early this morning. His woman, Sally, came in today in quite a state of panic. She said that Gareau was worried; that he knew someone was out to get him, going to try to kill him he said and now he's suddenly gone missing. She went looking for him in the woods and found his canoe drifting in the bayou and his hat was floating nearby." Thomas said nothing as he tried to make some sense of it, but before he could the sheriff added slyly, "Seems you boys was out there yesterday. She says you argued and it was right after that he run off. Now that makes you the prime suspects I would say."

"We talked to him alright and he was scared of someone, that's true, but it wasn't us. Besides we don't even know for sure that he's dead. He said he was going to disappear. Maybe this was a ruse on his part. The woman is in on it, trying to make everybody think he's dead."

The sheriff disregarded Thomas's remark and spoke past him, "Now you get down from there, boy, you is under arrest."

It was at this point that the lawyer intervened, "On what charge, sheriff?" Chambers knew nothing of the details surrounding Thomas's meeting with Gareau, but he was smart and resourceful. He was trained to quickly size up an argument and fashion a suitable response. Like a skilled musician sitting in with a strange band be was able to play his part perfectly.

"Now who the hell are you?"

"My name is Virgil Chambers. I am Mr. Hamrick's attorney."

"Well... I never..." the sheriff shook his head disdainfully and said defiantly, "Suspicion of murder, is that good enough?"

"I don't think it is, sheriff. There is no corpse or even any compelling reason to believe Gareau is dead. It's much more likely that he has staged this scene to affect his escape. You're just fishing."

"Well... it's a nice day for it wouldn't you say?"

"Have you ever heard of a Writ of Habeas Corpus, sheriff?"

The sheriff smiled. "Go see Judge Graham. He's right over at the courthouse. See if he'll give you one." The implication of collusion was unmistakable and Chambers was getting used to it. He believed that the sheriff knew better than to try to arrest a White man on such flimsy evidence and wanted to bring the Black man in so he could rough him up, maybe even get him to confess to something he didn't do or to implicate Thomas. His mind was fast processing clues and the idea also occurred to him that this could all be part of a wider plan to intimidate them into taking Sanford's low ball offer. He remembered that it was a sheriff who had witnessed the signing of the critical contract decades earlier. But, this couldn't possibly be the same man, or could it?

The lawyer's next remark began to shake the sheriff's confidence that he could bluff Chambers. "Any judge that willfully refuses to grant such a writ in so plainly blatant a case of the abuse of power such as this can be found guilty of a criminal offence and imprisoned. The war is over sheriff, here in Mississippi Habeas Corpus is no longer subject to the whim of government."

"I still say go see if you can get your damn writ," the sheriff responded, obviously out of ideas and showing a bit less arrogance.

"I don't need to go to your judge, sheriff," Chambers replied coolly, "I can go to any circuit judge anywhere in the state and believe me I'll have that writ before sundown and then I will bring an action against you for false imprisonment."

The sheriff didn't like being publicly challenged, especially by an uppity Black and began to show some anger. "And what if I just ignore you and your blasted writ, just for a couple of days mind you, until I get what I want."

"Try that sheriff and you will be made personally liable for the sum of one-thousand dollars payable to the person falsely imprisoned. That's the law sheriff; go ask your friend, the judge. Add to that the fact that you would be in contempt of court and... my judge... could put you behind bars."

The sheriff was seething, but only Uncle Henry correctly interpreted the danger in his faint smile. The old man was scared and his heart began to pound. In his mind he begged this young brother to reign in his sarcastic remarks. This wasn't a law school debate. This was the real world and there was sure to be a price to pay.

But, Chambers only saw the sheriff visibly reconsidering his options and was sure that this was little more than a clumsy heavy-handed attempt to pressure the Hamricks. So, seeing his adversary staggering he struck again. "The people of Mississippi remember the military occupation and what it meant to be powerless before the police authority. Habeas Corpus is a cherished right of all Mississippians and you're not going to sully it, sir. I suggest that you unhand this man immediately."

Then, just as he thought he had won and the sheriff was about to relent, Uncle Henry spoke. "I doan wan' no trouble. I be goin' along wit' de sheriff."

Chambers tried to advise him not to, but the old man didn't want to listen and told the lawyer, "I seed dat fancy talk befo'. Doan do nobody no good at de end uv a rope."

The two Black men were separated by more than age. They had had no common experience and almost no basis for understanding. They were in different worlds and there was no way to bridge that cavernous gap.

"This is the very reason that lynching occurs... because the law doesn't protect the Negro people," Chambers implored, his voice rising to reach the level of his emotional rhetoric. "It allows them to be murdered and nothing is done about it. The only defense is to apply the law equally and trust in the law to yield justice."

"I doan be no Negro people," Henry responded eloquently. "I be jus' one a de Negroes... but, I be de one dat gits lynched."

Amanda reacted at the news that Uncle Henry had been arrested. "He's what!"

"Shhhh, Mandy keep your voice down, these walls are paper thin," Thomas warned.

"For murder!" Lula almost shrieked.

"Please, ladies," Chambers added, "he's right. We really should modulate our voices."

Thomas then calmly recounted the details of Gareau's disappearance and explained that Uncle Henry had been taken in for questioning, but not to worry because they both believed that Gareau was scared and ran off and was not murdered at all. The lawyer's confident assurance that he would be released by evening seemed to calm them and Chambers set about to explain the plan to Mattie. Considering the personal risk she was being asked to take, he expected to meet resistance. But, she seemed to have passed a kind of breaking point and wanted to fight back.

"What do I have to do?"

"I have the papers right here for you to sign," the lawyer responded. "You just need to authorize me to represent you and I will serve them on Mrs. Hamrick right now."

It was a strangest kind of lawsuit, filed in a rented room between friends in an effort to acquire something they already knew to be almost worthless. But, that wasn't the point at all. It would provide leverage in any future negotiations with Dinkin Sanford. The lawyer smiled because he had the better information. His adversary didn't yet know that the river crossing had been rejected. If they acted quickly the tables could be turned.

"I think this calls for a celebration," Thomas said smiling.

"Let's not get ahead of ourselves," Chambers replied, "there's more to talk about."

The serious expression on the lawyer's face sobered the scene and they all sat to listen. "I thought about the so-called contract that supposedly gave Gareau an option to buy Grassy Water and I know it's bogus."

"Well I know it too," Thomas reacted. "Gareau admitted it to me, but he won't come forward so what good does that do us?"

"We don't need Gareau. I can prove it's a fake because it is dated 1833 and it specifically mentions the Mississippi Valuation and Debt Law." He paused for dramatic effect and finished, "that law was not enacted until 1840."

"Oh, my," Amanda reacted. "Well, we'll win then, won't we?"

"We can't reveal what we know until the trial or they'll just replace the document with a corrected one. And there's no way we can be sure to prevail at trial anyway because the case falls into the jurisdiction of the court here in Grenada, where we can't be sure of a fair shake. What we've got is leverage. I suggest we use it to con the conman. He thinks Grassy Water is worth a fortune and needs to act before you find out. Desperate men will do desperate things."

"But we know that the land is worthless." Thomas questioned.

"But, he doesn't. Don't you see? He'll be eager to get a deal done quickly... even if it costs him a lot more than he anticipated, it will be nothing compared to what it could cost him and what he thinks he'll make on the deal."

Amanda noticed the puzzled look on Mattie-Lou's face and it confirmed her own confusion. "I don't quite understand, Mr. Chambers."

"Look at it this way, Mrs. Hamrick. Sanford wants the land because he believes it will soon be worth a fortune. He used Gareau to concoct a scheme to give him an option to buy it from your brother's heirs at a price determined by the assessment of an appointed commission. That commission has met and at the moment that assessment makes the land virtually worthless, so his price is very low, which is what he wants. But, if it were to come out that a new railroad bridge was about to be built on it, you would rightfully demand a new assessment, the value would skyrocket and so would his price."

"So he's anxious to get the deal done before we find out what... he thinks... the land is really worth."

"Exactly! It's wise to realize that what is true is not as important as what people believe to be true," the lawyer philosophized.

"But, doesn't that put us in the same bind?" Thomas interjected. "I mean we have to get this done before he finds out the real truth or he won't bite."

"Indeed," the lawyer remarked, "but, we've got to act like we have all the time in world. That's why the threat to file for dower is perfect."

The lawyer's plan was not what Amanda had at first envisioned, but it was much more in keeping with what Lula seemed to want and it was so poetically just that she quickly came around.

"If you're clear now about what I am suggesting," Chambers said, "then with your permission I'll set up a meeting this afternoon with Sanford and his attorneys."

"Let's watch him drink his own poison," Amanda replied with a satisfied smile.

CHAPTER TWENTY-ONE

Dinkin Sanford and Claiborne Barr had been at the office with Graham Fly for some time before Thomas and his attorney arrived for the meeting. When he introduced Virgil Chambers all three men were visibly puzzled. Swift glances were exchanged, but no one spoke. Chambers smiled broadly and extended his hand, knowing that they needed the deal and would pretend not to notice that he was Black. "How do you do, gentlemen?"

Fly came quickly around his desk and enthusiastically shook Chambers' hand, "Graham Fly, pleased to meet you, sir. This is Mr. Dinkin Sanford and his attorney Claiborne Barr."

Barr reached out and shook Chambers' hand, but said nothing. Sanford looked up from his chair, nodded and then said to his lawyer, "Let's get on with it, Claiborne."

"Well... I think we'll all agree that the purpose of this meeting is to find an amicable way to expedite the transfer of the property. Mr. Sanford understands that certain hardships may be involved and he is prepared, as we have said previously, to extend, shall we say, certain considerations..." Barr paused briefly trying to interpret his client's apparent impatience. "... and... as I said... that is, the plantation known as Grassy Water, located on the north bank of the Yalobusha River at thirty-three degrees..."

"Sit down, Claiborne. I'll handle this." Sanford said tersely as he rose to his feet and then directly to Thomas added, "Let's just settle on a price, Hamrick, shall we. I don't have all day. We're not making a sales pitch here. We don't need to do this. It's just easier that's all."

"I'm not in a position to do that," Thomas responded, deciding to be deliberately annoying. "The property belongs to my wife."

"Damn it, man, she's your wife. Just tell her what the hell..."

Chambers saw the frown flash across Thomas's brow and interrupted before a destructive confrontation developed. "Mrs. Hamrick is at this moment in Grenada, at the Planter's Hotel and she is prepared to agree to the sale of Grassy Water to Mr. Sanford if a fair price can be reached. I am authorized to negotiate that amount and I can have her signature within the hour."

"The price has been determined by the assessment, according to law, at four thousand dollars," Claiborne Barr replied, "and as was previously stipulated, my client is prepared to add one thousand dollars in consideration for Mrs. Hamrick's timely signature. I believe this is a very generous offer."

"Too generous," Sanford grumbled as he returned to his chair.

Chambers placed his briefcase on the oak credenza, turned slowly and continued to by-pass Barr by speaking directly to Dinkin Sanford. "There are serious complications."

"What do you mean?" Barr replied, reasserting himself. "What kind of complications?"

"I am informing you that the decedent's widow, Mattie Prichard Olmstead, has filed a claim for dower."

"Dower, you can't be serious!"

"I am indeed, sir."

Once again, Sanford could no longer contain himself and interrupted, "What's going on here, Claiborne? What the hell is this dower?"

"Give us a minute," the lawyer remarked, without looking up while gathering some papers, and hastily ushered his client into the corridor.

For several minutes during their absence, Fly, continuing the subterfuge of neutrality, made several attempts to get more information. "What do you hope to gain, Chambers? You know damn well she'll lose. What's the point of this?"

"It's not my decision councilor. Mrs. Olmstead has a right to protect herself. She's being cut out of her rightful inheritance."

Fly turned to Thomas who had, with difficulty, disciplined himself to stay out of it. "As executor of the will I feel obligated to advise Mrs. Hamrick that she should deny this claim for dower and go ahead with the proposed sale. Let the courts sort it out later."

Thomas said nothing letting his attorney reply. Chambers handed the appropriate papers to Fly. "I'm afraid it's too late for that."

The lawyer's eyes ran quickly over the page. "She's already agreed to it? For God's sake not metes and bounds... how could you let her do that?"

A satisfied smile spread across Thomas's face when Virgil Chambers remarked caustically, "If you want to do a deal then drop the ruse. You're not fooling anyone." Fly could see immediately that he had been set up, but had no ready answers and Chambers added, gesturing with his thumb, "Now, why don't you join your friends in the hallway? I'm sure you'll have a lot to add to the conversation."

Fly could see that the ploy had failed and he could also tell that the real negotiation was about to begin. He decided to drop the pretense and left the office without saying another word. The three were gone for several more minutes leading Chambers to conclude, and Thomas agreed, that Sanford was now devising a new strategy. When the men returned neither Thomas nor his attorney was surprised when Sanford spoke for himself.

"Just what do you want, Hamrick?"

Once again Thomas needled Sanford by deferring to his attorney. "It's not about what Mr. Hamrick wants, Mr. Sanford. It's about protecting the interests of my clients by getting a fair price for the land."

Sanford could see his get-rich-quick scheme evaporating before his eyes. He knew that time was of the essence and he was angry at being stymied, especially by a Negro. He wanted to be rude, but realized that it was unlikely to help. The frustration was evident in his voice. "You've been offered a fair price. The assessment is proper." Then before Chambers could respond the con continued and Sanford, ever the sly fox, said, "But... to help the widow... I'll add another thousand. Six thousand dollars, Chambers, but that's as far as I will go." Then he turned to Thomas and added, "The damn place is worthless and you know it."

"Mrs. Olmstead will not accept that as she's entitled to one third of the land by metes and bounds; and she will sue to get it."

Sanford began to reply, but his lawyer prevented him and said, "This claim for dower will fail and you know it. My client will win in court and you'll get exactly what the assessment calls for. You're about to cost your clients two thousand dollars my friend and as far as I'm concerned we've made our final offer, take it or leave it." He looked at Sanford and the two men rose to their feet in a determined effort to look resolved.

"See you in court," Chambers quipped coolly, convinced that this was a bluff and as the two men marched toward the door, Fly proved him right. "Wait, gentlemen," he exclaimed loudly, standing and raising his hands. "Let me have a go at it."

"It's a waste of time, Graham," came the mock objection.

"Please, I have an idea."

"What have we got to lose," Barr said to Sanford, who feigned a grudging agreement. The two men slowly returned to their seats to listen to Fly's contrived proposal.

"Let's look at this realistically," he said directly to Thomas. "You wouldn't still be here if you weren't prepared to reach an agreement. This is all about money. How much do you want?"

"Talk to my lawyer," Thomas replied.

Chambers made no attempt to parry the claim that the right amount of cash could solve the impasse and responded directly with a figure. "Forty-thousand dollars."

Dead silence filled the space then suddenly Sanford reacted, utterly astounded by the number. "That's ten times the market value," he almost screamed. "What makes you think anyone would pay that?"

"Because this particular piece of land is worth double that," Chambers answered and then paused before continuing. "We know about the railroad bridge, gentlemen." He said it slowly in the tone of matter of fact disdain that a parent would use after catching a child in a lie.

The room fell silent again for several seconds. Neither Fly nor Barr was prepared to respond and when Barr began stammering an angry Dinkin Sanford took control. "Shut up, Claiborne. I'll handle this. Look Hamrick, what is it to you anyway? I'm going to get that land. If you give me a fair price then you'll make out too. I'll beat you in court and you'll lose some real money. Take your pick."

Again Thomas stayed silent and Chambers answered. "You may win the case for dower and eventually get your contract enforced, but I'll tie you up for months, maybe even years. You know as well as we that the army engineers are about to announce that the crossing at Grassy Water is sound. In a few days everyone else in Mississippi will know it too. When that happens, Mrs. Hamrick will demand a new assessment of the value of Grassy Water... and she'll get it. Then watch the price go up. You need to act now. Let's not waste each other's time any more. Make us a realistic offer."

"Two-thousand dollars to the widow...if she agrees to drop the claim for dower and ten-thousand for the land."

"Five and twenty..."

"Agreed... if it's done today."

They came from miles around, some on horseback or in wagons, but most of them walked. There were far too many to accommodate in the front parlor where the ceremony was to take place so, in a way ironically reminiscent of slave times, they gathered on the veranda to look in through the windows.

Granny Mo had saved flour and sugar for weeks to prepare the pastries that covered the long tables that had been set up in the shade under the big oak tree along the side yard. It seemed like everybody in the world wanted to be part of it and do something. Granny Mo was hard pressed to find enough cherries to pit, eggs to beat and butter to cream. They had worked well into the night before and had sung every song anyone could remember.

And now the time had finally arrived. The excitement was palpable and even the opening strains from the small piano announcing the impending entrance of the bride couldn't contain them. The windows were thrown open and the curtains pulled back. There was no more need to press noses against the glass.

Her gown was pure white and high cut. Her sleeves were long, befitting the solemnity of the occasion and she wore white satin slippers and gloves. A single strand of pearls fell lazily across her breast and on her brow was a circlet of exquisite white wax orange blossoms. At that moment she was the most beautiful of all brides.

The buzz on the veranda fell to a gasping hush. A woman's voice could clearly be heard saying, "I member dem weddins in de big ouse. Dey shu was fine... but dis here be de bestus of 'em all..."

Caleb squeezed Angeline's hand and she looked up at him. Her green eyes, burning through the filmy haze of the sheer silk veil that cascaded over her face, were stunning. He hardly heard anything after that.

"A reading from Corinthians," the Minster began and the crowd outside, straining to see and hear, pressed closer against the door and windows. Some voices filtered through the sound of breathing and the shifting of feet.

"Ain't it gran'! I members when dey jus' jumps backuds ober de broom."

"Shhh...'

"...we didin hab nuffin' but ebryday cloes."

"Shhh, I wants te listen..."

"...Love is patient, love is kind. It does not envy, it does not boast..."

"...my weddin' dress was real pretty too ..."

"Shhh..." came up all around her, but the woman was alone in her world of memories.

"...an white wit lace an bows..."

"...it is not proud. It is not rude, it is not self-seeking..."

"...it was de Mistus dress fore me..."

"...it is not easily angered; it keeps no record of wrongs. Love does not delight in evil, but rejoices with the truth..."

"...an she gib me de veil too..."

"...It always protects, always trusts, always hopes, always perseveres..."

"You hush now, dey's sayin' de words," a man in front ordered and seeing the hopeless expressions on the forlorn faces of those behind him assumed the role of a kind of announcer.

"I, Caleb, take thee, Angeline, to be my wife..."

"He be takin' her now..."

"...and before God and these witnesses I promise to be a faithful and true husband."

"...and now she gonna be takin' him..."

"I, Angeline, take thee, Caleb, to be my husband, and before God and these witnesses I promise to be a faithful and true wife."

"Now dey done tuk each udder..."

A raucous "Amen, Amen," streamed in from the veranda and mingled with some spontaneous applause from within that was quickly doused by the minister's stern look and loud voice.

"The rings please."

Fortunately, Aunt Effie had remembered to remove the stitches from the seam of the glove and the maid of honor rolled back the fabric on Angeline's finger.

"...with this ring I thee wed..."

He reached down and gently lifted her veil. Her flawless skin and radiant bronze complexion, bursting from the snowy sameness surrounding it, commanded every eye and stilled every breath.

"He be kissin' her now..."

The cheering on the veranda erupted before their lips met and spread like a contagion through the open windows engulfing them all. They hardly heard the minister say, "Ladies and gentlemen may I introduce Mr. and Mrs. Caleb Pritchard."

The frolic was destined to roll on and on through the night. The only remaining solemn moment came when Thomas made the toast. His words to the young couple were eloquent and inspiring, but then came the moment of unexpected sadness. It swept across the crowd cruelly wiping away the smiles and happy faces.

"For all of you who have called Grassy Water home, what I'm about to tell you may be difficult to bear. Some of you were born here and I know that many of you still live here." He paused briefly in the hope that there was some better way to say it that he hadn't yet thought of, but there wasn't. "The plantation has been sold."

It really wasn't a surprise. Everyone expected it, but when it finally came they were still unprepared and stood in stunned silence. A few seconds passed and when no one spoke, Thomas went on. "There is some good news though. The sale will provide a trust fund for Mattie, which should keep her comfortable for the rest of her life and a tidy sum in cash for Samuel's son, Caleb, enough for him and Angeline to start up again anywhere they choose."

The cheer of genuine happiness for another's good fortune at a time when they themselves faced homelessness brought tears to Thomas's eyes. But, there was nothing he could do. He couldn't save them... except for one. "Not parts of the sale are a mare, two mules and a wagon. These now belong to the man who loves them the most."

Another raucous cheer rose up and everyone turned to look at Uncle Henry who was waiting along the drive with the wedding carriage. Thomas said some more words, but he couldn't be heard above the tumultuous celebration that simply refused to die away. It was the perfect moment for the couple to depart on their wedding trip. Uncle Henry was waiting to take them to Grenada where the train to Vicksburg would connect them with a steamboat to New Orleans. Jim Crow hadn't yet climbed aboard the steamboats and New Orleans seemed very far away, mysterious and fun.

The surrey worked wonderfully for a wedding carriage. The bride's maids had spent hours tying white ribbons and bows all over it and weaving jasmine and roses wherever a crack could be found. It was splendid to see and would match the equipage of any Russian Czar.

The old man had fussed all morning with his team. He knew that the pair was as important as the carriage and although he didn't have fancy matching stallions he now owned the prettiest mules that God ever made. They were tall for mollies, a full sixteen hands and as identical as twins, cinnamon red and sweet as sugar. Ears up tall and tight together, eyes twinkling in the sunshine they were smart enough to know the honor they had been given.

The old man himself was spruced up beyond what anyone, even Granny Tine, could recall. It made everyone smile to see him dressed in the woolen full double-breasted frock coat, top hat and brand new boots that "Marsta" Sam never got to wear.

Uncle Henry was as happy as anyone had ever seen him. He climbed to his seat in the surrey and steadied the mules with a soft word as the crowd pressed in on the carriage to get a last glimpse of the newlyweds and just before departing turned to them and said with the wisdom of Moses, “We only be here fer a spell, an mossa de time whilst we young we doan see how tings be shiftin’.”

Epilog

Dear Anna,

I'm so glad that I finally found your address, there's so much that I want to tell you. Of course the railroad bridge was never built and Sanford's scheme fell apart. Grassy Water sat idle for a long time after that. I guess he was hoping that something would change, but it didn't. When the new rail route was set well east of us, Sanford finally tried to sell it, but there were no buyers.

He never pushed the people out because at least they were keeping the place from falling down. So nothing really changed until about six months ago when we saw an announcement that the land was going to be auctioned off in Natchez. It seemed so ironic, being Natchez and all, and we talked about it, but I never dreamed that Caleb would want it. Anyway, he went and bid five-hundred dollars. It was a laughably low bid, meant more as an insult I think, but it was the only bid. Sanford didn't have to take it. He looked at Caleb for a long time. I guess he was desperate.

Please be sure to tell Aunt Amanda that Caleb is now master of Grassy Water and that his mother and Aunt Effie are back with us. Everybody's excited and working hard. They're opening up a lot of the back woodland and lumber prices are very good right now. It's going to be hard, but Caleb thinks we can make a go of it and I do too. I know she'll be very pleased seeing as she came all this way to make that happen and now it finally did. Tell her too that we all love her and miss her and that Uncle Henry never stops talking about her and Uncle Thomas.

Now that you know where we are please write soon.

Love always, your cousin,
Angeline

Grassy Water, Mississippi
October 1885